NATIONAL ACADEMIES *Sciences Engineering Medicine*

NATIONAL ACADEMIES PRESS
Washington, DC

Cybercrime Classification and Measurement

Hal S. Stern and Daniel L. Cork,
Editors

Panel on Cybercrime Classification and Measurement

Committee on National Statistics

Committee on Law and Justice

Division of Behavioral and Social Sciences and Education

Computer Science and Telecommunications Board

Division on Engineering and Physical Sciences

Consensus Study Report

NATIONAL ACADEMIES PRESS 500 Fifth Street, NW Washington, DC 20001

This activity was supported by a contract between the National Academy of Sciences and the Federal Bureau of Investigation, U.S. Department of Justice, Contract No. 15F06723C0001869. Any opinions, findings, conclusions, or recommendations expressed in this publication do not necessarily reflect the views of any organization or agency that provided support for the project.

International Standard Book Number-13: 978-0-309- 73461-5
Digital Object Identifier: https://doi.org/10.17226/29048
Library of Congress Control Number: 2025938656

This publication is available from the National Academies Press, 500 Fifth Street, NW, Keck 360, Washington, DC 20001; (800) 624-6242; https://nap.nationalacademies.org.

The manufacturer's authorized representative in the European Union for product safety is Authorised Rep Compliance Ltd., Ground Floor, 71 Lower Baggot Street, Dublin D02 P593 Ireland; www.arccompliance.com.

Copyright 2025 by the National Academy of Sciences. National Academies of Sciences, Engineering, and Medicine and National Academies Press and the graphical logos for each are all trademarks of the National Academy of Sciences. All rights reserved.

Printed in the United States of America.

Suggested citation: National Academies of Sciences, Engineering, and Medicine. 2025. *Cybercrime Classification and Measurement*. Washington, DC: National Academies Press. https://doi.org/10.17226/29048.

The **National Academy of Sciences** was established in 1863 by an Act of Congress, signed by President Lincoln, as a private, nongovernmental institution to advise the nation on issues related to science and technology. Members are elected by their peers for outstanding contributions to research. Dr. Marcia McNutt is president.

The **National Academy of Engineering** was established in 1964 under the charter of the National Academy of Sciences to bring the practices of engineering to advising the nation. Members are elected by their peers for extraordinary contributions to engineering. Dr. John L. Anderson is president.

The **National Academy of Medicine** (formerly the Institute of Medicine) was established in 1970 under the charter of the National Academy of Sciences to advise the nation on medical and health issues. Members are elected by their peers for distinguished contributions to medicine and health. Dr. Victor J. Dzau is president.

The three Academies work together as the **National Academies of Sciences, Engineering, and Medicine** to provide independent, objective analysis and advice to the nation and conduct other activities to solve complex problems and inform public policy decisions. The National Academies also encourage education and research, recognize outstanding contributions to knowledge, and increase public understanding in matters of science, engineering, and medicine.

Learn more about the National Academies of Sciences, Engineering, and Medicine at **www.nationalacademies.org**.

Consensus Study Reports published by the National Academies of Sciences, Engineering, and Medicine document the evidence-based consensus on the study's statement of task by an authoring committee of experts. Reports typically include findings, conclusions, and recommendations based on information gathered by the committee and the committee's deliberations. Each report has been subjected to a rigorous and independent peer-review process and it represents the position of the National Academies on the statement of task.

Proceedings published by the National Academies of Sciences, Engineering, and Medicine chronicle the presentations and discussions at a workshop, symposium, or other event convened by the National Academies. The statements and opinions contained in proceedings are those of the participants and are not endorsed by other participants, the planning committee, or the National Academies.

Rapid Expert Consultations published by the National Academies of Sciences, Engineering, and Medicine are authored by subject-matter experts on narrowly focused topics that can be supported by a body of evidence. The discussions contained in rapid expert consultations are considered those of the authors and do not contain policy recommendations. Rapid expert consultations are reviewed by the institution before release.

For information about other products and activities of the National Academies, please visit www.nationalacademies.org/about/whatwedo.

PANEL ON CYBERCRIME CLASSIFICATION AND MEASUREMENT

HAL S. STERN (*Chair*), Distinguished Professor of Statistics, University of California, Irvine
LYNN A. ADDINGTON, Professor of Justice, Law, and Criminology, American University
ERICA R. FISSEL, Research and Evaluation Manager, ICF, Tallahassee, Florida
THOMAS J. HOLT, Professor in the School of Criminal Justice, Michigan State University
JIN REE LEE, Assistant Professor in the Department of Criminology, Law, and Society, George Mason University
DAVID MAIMON, Professor in the Department of Criminal Justice and Criminology, Georgia State University
MARIE-HELEN (MARIA) MARAS, Professor in the Center for Cybercrime Studies, John Jay College of Criminal Justice
MICHAEL C. MILLER, Chief of Police, Colleyville, Texas
OJMARRH MITCHELL, Professor of Criminology, Law, and Society, University of California, Irvine
ALEXIS R. PIQUERO, Professor of Sociology and Criminology, University of Miami
STACEY A. WRIGHT, Director of Cyber Threat Intelligence, CyberWA, New York

Study Staff

DANIEL L. CORK, Study Director
ANTHONY S. MANN, Senior Program Associate
KATRINA BAUM STONE, Senior Program Officer
EMILY BACKES, Deputy Director, Committee on Law and Justice
THO NGUYEN, Senior Program Officer, Computer Science and Telecommunications Board

Consultant

ADAM DEAN, New York State Division of Criminal Justice Services

COMMITTEE ON NATIONAL STATISTICS

KATHARINE G. ABRAHAM (*Chair*), Distinguished University Professor of Economics, University of Maryland, College Park
MICK P. COUPER, Research Professor Emeritus, University of Michigan
WILLIAM (SANDY) A. DARITY, JR., Samuel DuBois Cook Distinguished Professor of Public Policy, Duke University
ROBERT M. GOERGE, Senior Research Fellow, NORC at the University of Chicago
ERICA L. GROSHEN, Senior Labor Market Advisor, Cornell University
ROEE GUTMAN, Professor of Biostatistics, Brown University
COLLEEN M. HEFLIN, Professor of Public Administration and International Affairs, Syracuse University
DANIEL E. HO, William Benjamin Scott and Luna M. Scott Professor of Law, Stanford Law School
HILARY W. HOYNES, Chancellor's Professor of Economics and Public Policy, University of California, Berkeley
HOSAGRAHAR V. JAGADISH, Edgar F. Codd Distinguished University Professor, University of Michigan
SHARON LOHR, Emeritus Professor, Arizona State University
LLOYD B. POTTER, Texas State Demographer, University of Texas at San Antonio
NELA RICHARDSON, Chief Economist, ADP Research Institute
ELIZABETH A. STUART, Frank Hurley and Catharine Dorrier Professor, Johns Hopkins Bloomberg School of Public Health
FLORENCIA TORCHE, Edwards S. Sanford Professor of International Affairs and Sociology, Princeton University
SALIL VADHAN, Vicky Joseph Professor of Computer Science and Applied Mathematics, Harvard University

Staff

MELISSA CHIU, Director
CONSTANCE F. CITRO, Senior Scholar
BRIAN HARRIS-KOJETIN, Senior Scholar

COMMITTEE ON LAW AND JUSTICE

ROBERT D. CRUTCHFIELD (*Chair*), Professor Emeritus of Sociology, University of Washington
JOHN M. MACDONALD (*Vice Chair*), Professor of Criminology and Sociology, University of Pennsylvania
MONICA C. BELL, Professor of Law, Yale Law School
ANTHONY A. BRAGA, Jerry Lee Professor of Criminology, University of Pennsylvania
ROD K. BRUNSON, Professor in the Department of Criminology and Criminal Justice, University of Maryland, College Park
ELSA Y. CHEN, Professor in the Department of Political Science, Santa Clara University
JENS LUDWIG, Edwin A. and Betty L. Bergman Distinguished Service Professor, University of Chicago
SAMUEL L. MYERS, JR., Professor in the Hubert H. Humphrey School of Public Affairs, University of Minnesota
EMILY OWENS, Deans' Professor of Criminology and Economics, University of California, Irvine
ALEXIS R. PIQUERO, Professor of Sociology and Criminology, University of Miami
JESENIA PIZARRO, Professor in the School of Criminology and Criminal Justice, Arizona State University
LAURIE O. ROBINSON, Clarence J. Robinson Professor of Criminology, Law, and Society, George Mason University
ADDIE C. ROLNICK, San Manuel Professor of Law, University of Nevada, Las Vegas
VINCENT SCHIRALDI, Secretary of Maryland Department of Juvenile Services
CHRISTOPHER UGGEN, Regents Professor, University of Minnesota
EMILY A. WANG, Professor in the Yale School of Medicine and Public Health, Yale University

Staff

NATACHA BLAIN, Director
EMILY BACKES, Deputy Director

COMPUTER SCIENCE AND TELECOMMUNICATIONS BOARD

LAURA M. HAAS (*Chair*), Donna M. and Robert J. Manning Dean, University of Massachusetts, Amherst
DAVID DANKS, Professor of Data Science & Philosophy, University of California, San Diego
CHARLES LEE ISBELL, JR., Provost and Vice Chancellor for Academic Affairs, University of Wisconsin–Madison
ECE KAMAR, Partner Research Area Manager, Microsoft Research, Redmond, Washington
JAMES F. KUROSE, Distinguished Professor Emeritus, University of Massachusetts, Amherst
DAVID LUEBKE, Vice President of Graphics Research, NVIDIA
DAWN C. MEYERRIECKS, Senior Visiting Fellow, MITRE Corporation
WILLIAM L. SCHERLIS, Professor of Software and Societal Systems, Carnegie Mellon University
HENNING G. SCHULZRINNE, Julian Clarence Levi Professor of Mathematical Methods and Computer Science, Columbia University
NAMBIRAJAN SESHADRI, Professor of Practice, University of California, San Diego
KENNETH E. WASHINGTON, Senior Vice President and Chief Technology and Innovation Officer, Medtronic
JOHN L. MANFERDELLI, Independent Consultant (*ex officio member*)

Staff

JON EISENBERG, Director

Reviewers

This Consensus Study Report was reviewed in draft form by individuals chosen for their diverse perspectives and technical expertise. The purpose of this independent review is to provide candid and critical comments that will assist the National Academies of Sciences, Engineering, and Medicine in making each published report as sound as possible and to ensure that it meets the institutional standards for quality, objectivity, evidence, and responsiveness to the study charge. The review comments and draft manuscript remain confidential to protect the integrity of the deliberative process.

We thank the following individuals for their review of this report:

GEORGE W. BURRUSS, Department of Criminology and the Cybercrime Interdisciplinary Behavioral Research Laboratory, University of South Florida
KYUNG-SHICK CHOI, Cybercrime Investigation & Cybersecurity Graduate Programs, Boston University
SUSAN PADDOCK, NORC at the University of Chicago
GREG RIDGEWAY, Department of Criminology, University of Pennsylvania
STEFAN SAVAGE, Department of Computer Science and Engineering, University of California, San Diego
JEFFREY D. ULLMAN, Department of Computer Science, Stanford University

Although the reviewers listed above provided many constructive comments and suggestions, they were not asked to endorse the conclusions or recommendations of this report, nor did they see the final draft before its release. The review of this report was overseen by **JAMES P. LYNCH,** Department of Criminology and Criminal Justice, University of Maryland, and **DOUGLAS S. MASSEY,** Department of Sociology, Princeton University. They were responsible for making certain that an independent examination of this report was carried out in accordance with the standards of the National Academies and that all review comments were carefully considered. Responsibility for the final content rests entirely with the authoring panel and the National Academies.

Acknowledgments

The Panel on Cybercrime Classification and Measurement is pleased to submit this final report, and we are deeply thankful to all participants who contributed to our work.

Foremost, we appreciate the support and diligence of the project's sponsor, the Criminal Justice Information Services (CJIS) Division of the Federal Bureau of Investigation (FBI), U.S. Department of Justice. We benefited from our interactions with Edward Abraham, unit chief. Amy Snider began as the panel's lead contact within CJIS until her retirement, when Drema Fouch added liaison work with our panel to her Uniform Crime Reporting (UCR) Program duties; they were both great partners in this work.

Though the Bureau of Justice Statistics (BJS) was not a formal sponsor of our study, BJS remained a deeply interested party, commensurate with its joint sponsorship with CJIS of our predecessor Panel on Modernizing the Nation's Crime Statistics. In particular, this panel benefited greatly from regular interactions with BJS staff members Rachel Morgan, Erica Smith, and Erika Harrell over the course of our information-gathering sessions.

The project's schedule was such that our members and invited speakers alike had to support a grueling back-to-back series of information-gathering public sessions in quick succession in April–June 2024. In addition to the already mentioned Edward Abraham, Drema Fouch, and Rachel Morgan, we express our thanks to the speakers who contributed to our public meetings on short notice:

- Mary Aiken and Julia Davidson, Institute for Connected Communities, University of East London;

- Detective First Lieutenant James Ellis and Lieutenant Gordon Armstrong, Michigan Cyber Command Center, Computer Crimes Unit, Michigan State Police;
- Mark Fetterhoff, AARP;
- Emma Fletcher, Federal Trade Commission;
- Lauren Boas Hayes, Cybersecurity & Infrastructure Security Agency, U.S. Department of Homeland Security;
- Matt LaVigna, National Cyber-Forensics and Training Alliance;
- Lawrence (Wes) Quigley, Internet Crime Complaint Center, FBI;
- Warren Silver and Julie Sauvé, Statistics Canada;
- Joan Smith, Washington Association of Sheriffs and Police Chiefs (on behalf of the Association of State Uniform Crime Reporting Programs); and
- Eva Velasquez and James Lee, Identity Theft Resource Center.

The panel's work was greatly aided by its principal staff from the Committee on National Statistics (CNSTAT). As study director, Daniel Cork brought to bear his deep experience leading the predecessor Panel on Modernizing the Nation's Crime Statistics (as well as the Panel to Review the Programs of the Bureau of Justice Statistics) among other studies of the decennial census and federal statistics, and we benefited from his drafting of the panel's work. Dan's steady hand and resolute commitment allowed the panel to address its charge while adhering to a challenging timeline. Katrina Baum Stone contributed to the panel's discussion by drawing from her experience of previous work at BJS, including developmental work on several of the cybercrime-related supplements to the National Crime Victimization Survey. Anthony Mann provided smooth logistical support to the panel's operations, particularly in the fast-paced round of public sessions, while CNSTAT director Melissa Chiu provided important overall direction to the panel's work. Emily Backes, deputy director of the Committee on Law and Justice, participated in several panel meetings and stepped in to draft some background materials, while Tho Nguyen from the Computer Science and Telecommunications Board provided input during the panel formation and scoping process.

All members of the panel contributed their keen insights over a hectic series of meetings, and the group produced a remarkable sense of camaraderie despite having to do much of its work through virtual communications. We are particularly grateful to Adam Dean, deputy commissioner of operations and innovation at the New York State Division of Criminal Justice Services, for serving as an unpaid consultant to the panel, allowing him to contribute his knowledge as a state law enforcement practitioner while also continuing his role as chair of the UCR subcommittee of the FBI CJIS Advisory Policy Board. His perspective was a great asset to our

ACKNOWLEDGMENTS

discussions, and we look forward to further discussion on implementing improved cybercrime metrics.

Hal S. Stern, *Chair*
Panel on Cybercrime Classification and Measurement
April 2025

Contents

Acronyms and Abbreviations   xix

Summary   1

1   Introduction: Cybercrime Measurement, the Panel, and Its Charge   17
THE PANEL AND ITS CHARGE, 19
INTERPRETING THE CHARGE: THE CHALLENGES OF
    CLASSIFYING AND MEASURING CYBERCRIME, 21
ORGANIZATION OF THE REPORT, 26

2   Treatment of Cybercrime in Current Data Collections   29
CYBERCRIME HANDLING IN THE NATIONAL INCIDENT-
    BASED REPORTING SYSTEM, 29
CYBERCRIME HANDLING IN THE NATIONAL CRIME
    VICTIMIZATION SURVEY AND ITS SUPPLEMENTS, 41
OTHER ENTITIES COLLECTING CYBERCRIME-RELATED
    DATA, PARTICULARLY FRAUD, 57
COLLECTION OF CYBERSECURITY INCIDENT
    INFORMATION AND CYBERCRIME-RELATED
    INFORMATION FROM BUSINESS AND INDUSTRY, 64
EMERGING COLLECTIONS OF CYBERSECURITY AND
    CYBERCRIME-RELATED INCIDENTS, 66

INTERNATIONAL PARALLELS: CYBERCRIME DATA
COLLECTION IN CANADA, 75

3 Approaches to Cybercrime Classification   77
   CYBER-SPECIFIC TAXONOMIES: CYBERCRIME IN
      ISOLATION, 77
   CYBERCRIME IN CONTEXT OF ALL-CRIME
      TAXONOMIES, 80
   RECOMMENDED CLASSIFICATION OF CYBERCRIME, 84

4 Recommendations and Implementation Challenges   89
   CALIBRATE EXPECTATIONS: MARKERS OF CYBERCRIME,
      NOT EXACT MEASUREMENT, 89
   MEASURING CYBERCRIME BY LEVERAGING EXISTING
      DATA-COLLECTION EFFORTS, 90
   ASPIRATIONAL GOALS FOR CYBERCRIME
      MEASUREMENT, 95

References   101

Appendix A: Recent Federal Law on Cybercrime Classification   107

Appendix B: Detailed Definitions and Inclusions, Panel's
   Recommended Classification of Cybercrime   113

Appendix C: Cybercrime Offenses Defined in Current Systems
   and Law   121

Appendix D: Biographical Sketches of Panel Members and
   Principal Staff   131

Boxes, Figures, and Tables

BOXES

1-1 Statement of Task, 20

2-1 Crime Classification in the Uniform Crime Reporting Summary Reporting System, 30
2-2 Crime Classification in the National Crime Victimization Survey, 2017, 44
2-3 Response Options for Why Incident Was Not Reported to Law Enforcement, 2017 Supplemental Fraud Survey and 2021 Identity Theft Supplement, 48
2-4 Question 1, Types of Stalking Behaviors Measured, Supplemental Victimization Survey, 2019, 52
2-5 Types of Computer Security Incidents Covered by the 2005 National Computer Security Survey, 56
2-6 Response Options on Reporting and Nonreporting of Computer Security Incidents, 2005 National Computer Security Survey, 58
2-7 Report Categories in the Federal Trade Commission Consumer Sentinel Network, 62
2-8 Covered Threat Actions in the Vocabulary for Event Recording and Incident Sharing Framework, 67
2-9 Required Information for Covered Cyberincident Reports under the Cyber Incident Reporting for Critical Infrastructure Act, 73

3-1 Basic Cybercrime Types Identified in the Budapest Convention on Cybercrime (2001) and the Draft United Nations Convention on Cybercrime (August 2024), 80

FIGURES

S-1 Schematic of proposed classification of cybercrime, 9

2-1 Computer crime questions on the National Crime Victimization Survey, 2001–2004, 46

3-1 Schematic of proposed classification of cybercrime, 85

TABLES

2-1 National Incident-Based Reporting System Offense Codes, 34
2-2 Participation in National Incident-Based Reporting System by Law Enforcement Agencies, 2021–2022, 37
2-3 Current Use of Computer-Related Indicators in National Incident-Based Reporting System, 2022, 39
2-4 Overview of Cybercrime-Related Supplements to the National Crime Victimization Survey, 47
2-5 Victim Count in Crime Types Reported in Internet Crime Complaint Center Annual Reports, 2018–2023, 60

Acronyms and Abbreviations

BCMA	Better Cybercrime Metrics Act; P.L. 117-116
BJS	Bureau of Justice Statistics
CCC	Cybercrime Classification Compendium
CCJCSS	Canadian Centre for Justice and Community Safety Statistics
CDC	U.S. Centers for Disease Control and Prevention
CFAA	Computer Fraud and Abuse Act
CIRC	Cyber Incident Reporting Council
CIRCIA	Cyber Incident Reporting for Critical Infrastructure Act
CISA	Cybersecurity & Infrastructure Security Agency
DBIR	[Verizon] Data Breach Investigations Report
FBI	Federal Bureau of Investigation
FISMA	Federal Information Security Modernization Act
FTC	Federal Trade Commission
GQ	group quarters
IC3	Internet Crime Complaint Center [of the FBI]
ICCS	International Classification of Crime for Statistical Purposes
ICT	information and communication technology
ISAC	Information Sharing and Analysis Center

ISAO	Information Sharing and Analysis Organization
ITS	Identity Theft Supplement
MNCS panel	Panel on Modernizing the Nation's Crime Statistics
NCFTA	National Cyber-Forensics and Training Alliance
NCSS	National Computer Security Survey
NCVS	National Crime Victimization Survey
NIBRS	National Incident-Based Reporting System [of the FBI UCR Program]
NPRM	notice of proposed rulemaking
RMS	records management systems
SCS	School Crime Supplement [to the NCVS]
SEC	Securities and Exchange Commission
SFS	Supplemental Fraud Survey
SLTT	state, local, tribal, and territorial [as descriptor of law enforcement agencies]
SRS	Summary Reporting System [predecessor of NIBRS as UCR flagship collection]
SVS	Supplemental Victimization Survey [to the NCVS]
UCR	Uniform Crime Reporting [Program, of the FBI; Survey of Statistics Canada]
UN	United Nations
UNODC	United Nations Office on Drugs and Crime
USDHS	U.S. Department of Homeland Security
USDOJ	U.S. Department of Justice
USGAO	U.S. Government Accountability Office
VAWA	Violence Against Women Act
VERIS	Vocabulary for Event Recording and Incident Sharing

Summary

Cybercrime poses serious threats and financial costs to individuals and businesses in the United States and worldwide. Reports of data breaches and ransomware attacks on governments and businesses have become common, as have incidents of identity theft and online stalking and harassment against individuals. Concern over cybercrime has increased as the internet has become a ubiquitous part of modern life. However, the U.S. national crime statistics system has limited coverage of cybercrime, and existing measurement and data efforts to track such crimes are fragmented and hampered by challenges such as underreporting, the variable scope and nature of incidents, and the rapidly evolving nature of technology.

In response to these issues, two recent laws directly call for the addition of cybercrime content to current U.S. national crime statistics. Both of these laws—cybercrime provisions in the Violence Against Women Act Reauthorization Act of 2022 (P.L. 117-103) and the Better Cybercrime Metrics Act (BCMA; P.L. 117-116)[1]—require the Federal Bureau of Investigation (FBI) to add a category for cybercrime and cyber-enabled crime to the National Incident-Based Reporting System (NIBRS), the compilation of crime incident reports from thousands of state, local, tribal, and territorial (SLTT) law enforcement agencies. The BCMA expanded the focus

---

[1] See 136 Stat. 950 in P.L. 117-103 in particular, as P.L. 117-103 is the sprawling omnibus appropriations act for fiscal year 2002 into which numerous other bills were folded, including both the Violence Against Women Act Reauthorization Act and the Cyber Incident Reporting for Critical Infrastructure Act that is also a major focus in this study; both cybercrime reporting provisions are reprinted in Appendix A.

to cybercrimes against both individuals and businesses (rather than only individuals) and further directed the Bureau of Justice Statistics (BJS) to add cybercrime questions to the National Crime Victimization Survey (NCVS), the household survey that provides information on victimization incidents against individuals regardless of whether they were reported to police.

The BCMA also directed the U.S. Department of Justice to enter into an agreement with the National Academies of Sciences, Engineering, and Medicine (National Academies) to convene this Panel on Cybercrime Classification and Measurement, which it did through the FBI. The charge to the panel, shown in Chapter 1, was to develop a taxonomy to facilitate improved collection of cybercrime data in the nation's crime statistics system. In this task and in many important respects, our study is a direct extension of the predecessor Panel on Modernizing the Nation's Crime Statistics (hereafter, MNCS panel; National Academies, 2016a, 2018) that was jointly sponsored by the BJS and the FBI.

THE CHALLENGES OF CLASSIFYING AND MEASURING CYBERCRIME

A U.S. Government Accountability Office (2023; USGAO) review described an exceedingly decentralized web of at least 13 federal agencies with some responsibility for gathering information on cybercrime, including those tasked with the identification, investigation, and prosecution of cybercrime activity. The USGAO's overview of this data-collection terrain suggested wide variety in the manner, extent, and capability of these agencies to track cybercrime. Importantly, the review identified fundamental challenges to cybercrime data collection, among them the lack of common, consistent definitions of cybercrime; the lack of any integrative mechanism to combine and analyze results; and the lack of incentive among cybercrime victims to report incidents. In approaching our statement of task, we first described basic precepts guiding our work, focusing on the fit of "cybercrime" within the existing national crime statistics apparatus. One such precept is stated as a formal conclusion to motivate the work: the nature of cybercrime makes it inherently difficult to fit within the current national crime statistics system. For example, the "cyber" component of cybercrime offenses could be characterized as the victim, offender, modus operandi, location, motive, or weapon used in the offense logged in U.S. crime statistics. Moreover, the boundaries of cybercrime incidents can be difficult to pinpoint relative to the offense types covered in current statistics; data breaches and ransomware attacks can have ripple effects on thousands or millions of individuals, raising the concern of whether it is fair to count the affected data holder as the sole victim.

Conclusion 1-1: Measurement of cybercrime is challenging—particularly in the context of current U.S. national crime statistics—for a number of reasons, including expected underreporting, the variable scope and nature of incidents, and the changing nature of technology.

Two other precepts stem from the interpretation of the word "cybercrime" itself. First, the statement of task obliges us to be "crime"-centric in nature, conceptualizing "cybercrime" as crime with a cyber/computer component rather than as cyberactivity with a criminal component. Practically, this means that the language of federal and state criminal codes remains a necessary anchoring point: an essential part of the definition of crime (and cybercrime) is that it is unlawful behavior rather than simply bad or undesirable behavior. A related precept extends the counterpart cyberactivity-with-criminal-component approach, emphasizing that cybercrime and cybersecurity incidents or breaches are strongly related but not equivalent concepts. Many cybersecurity incidents, being conducted with malicious intent, are indeed cybercrimes, but such incidents may also arise from simple human or technological error or as a direct consequence of environmental/physical factors. Hence, while these concepts overlap significantly, not automatically equating the two is vital.

TREATMENT OF CYBERCRIME IN CURRENT DATA COLLECTIONS

Before developing our taxonomy for measuring cybercrime, we briefly reviewed the ways in which cybercrime and related concepts are measured in existing and developing data systems, with particular eye to the categorization schemes used in those systems.

National Crime Statistics: The National Incident-Based Reporting System and the National Crime Victimization Survey

Although the NIBRS format has been in development and available to SLTT law enforcement agencies since the late 1980s, it only became the centerpiece of the FBI's Uniform Crime Reporting (UCR) Program in January 2021, following retirement of the previous Summary Reporting System (SRS). Prior to 2021, the SRS provided no mechanism for coding cybercrime in the collection's core set of offenses known to police.[2] Adoption of the NIBRS format greatly expanded the roster of covered offenses including the cybercrime-related offenses of wire fraud and credit card fraud as

---

[2] It was technically possible to log cybercrime as a type of fraud or as "all other offenses," but in either case, the reporting was an arrests-only count.

subcategories of fraud; in 2013, NIBRS documentation formally revised the definition of wire fraud to include computers, email, text messages, and related technologies as the delivery mechanism. From NIBRS's inception, its Data Element 8 has provided a means for indicating computer involvement in any type of crime, asking whether the offender was suspected of using "Computer Equipment" in the crime. In 2015, the UCR Program took three major steps to improving cybercrime coverage, adding two new entries—Hacking/Computer Invasion and Identity Theft—as new crime types and adding Cyberspace as a response option for the location of the offense. However, these two existing indicators in NIBRS have challenges as true markers of cybercrime; the most recent NIBRS user manual documentation has modified the Data Element 8 response to "Computer Equipment (Handheld Devices)" and apparently intends to capture incidences of driving while texting, while the Cyberspace location definition focuses on internet involvement in the offense rather than computer involvement more generally.

The core NCVS, operated by BJS with the U.S. Census Bureau as data-collection agent, is a panel household survey in which an NCVS-2 Crime Incident Report interview is conducted for each victimization incident reported during the preceding six months, as elicited through the NCVS-1 Basic Screen Questionnaire. Historically, the NCVS has largely mirrored the definitions and concepts used in the UCR Program, precisely to estimate the extent of crime that is not reported to police through comparison with the UCR's police report numbers. Accordingly, core NCVS content largely mirrors the street crime/interpersonal crime focus of the historical UCR SRS and thus lacks obvious connection to cybercrime. However, the NCVS has long expanded its substantive reach through periodic fielding of supplemental questionnaires, which may be administered even if the household has no traditional violent crime to report. Over the years, NCVS supplements have permitted the survey program to touch on aspects of cybercrime: identity theft and fraud through the Identity Theft Supplement and Supplemental Fraud Survey, cyberstalking through the Supplemental Victimization Survey, and cyberbullying through the School Crime Supplement.

Other Entities Collecting Cybercrime-Related Data, Particularly Fraud

The FBI's Internet Crime Complaint Center (IC3), originally founded as the Internet Fraud Complaint Center, has the primary function of serving as a public front door to report internet-facilitated crimes. Though numerous variants of fraud dominate the listings in IC3's reports, other cybercrime types including ransomware, crimes against children, and harassment/stalking are reported to the IC3 by the public. As with the NIBRS, there is no underlying taxonomic structure to the IC3's list of covered offenses, save that the list is revised slightly from year to year based on increasing or decreasing frequency of particular offenses. Similarly, the Federal Trade Commission (FTC) populates its Consumer Sentinel Network database based on reports from the public through its online portal. While the IC3 has expanded its scope to include other types of cybercrime, the FTC's collection remains focused on fraud, currently including 20 main categories and 47 subcategories. Its internal categorizations specific to fraud are based principally on the object of value targeted by the fraud, but the categories are not generally filtered or constrained to focus on cybercrime.

Collection of Cybersecurity Incident Information and Cybercrime-Related Information from Business and Industry

Information Sharing and Analysis Centers (ISACs) and Information Sharing and Analysis Organizations (ISAOs) are nonprofit organizations intended to serve as trusted entities for information sharing on cybersecurity and cyberthreats. ISACs are specific to particular business/industry sectors falling under the general heading of critical infrastructure, while ISAOs are more flexible in their membership. The National Cyber-Forensics and Training Alliance (NCFTA) performs a similar function of bridging private industry and domestic/international law enforcement partners to foster a trusted, neutral environment for collaboration, with the incentive of working toward shared solutions. For purposes of this study, ISACs/ISAOs and the NCFTA provide useful models for promoting a culture of information sharing across industry and government, even though data products are not yet a part of their role.

The Verizon Data Breach Investigations Report (DBIR) is an annual report series, compiled since 2008 by Verizon Business and its Verizon Threat Research Advisory Center team, based on the voluntary submission of cybersecurity incident data from an evolving set of contributors. Data for the DBIR exist in a specific coding schema known as the Vocabulary for Event Recording and Incident Sharing (VERIS) which—though not a classic hierarchically structured taxonomy—provides a structured way of deconstructing cybersecurity events along four dimensions: Assets, Attributes, Actors, and Actions. Of these, VERIS's list of threat Actions is closest to a cybercrime classification scheme, containing five varieties that are highly relevant: Malware, Hacking, Social Engineering, Misuse of Assets, and Physical Actions.

Emerging Collections of Cybersecurity and Cybercrime-Related Incidents

The reporting of major cybersecurity incidents—many of which may be cybercrimes—is currently in a state of major change. The Cybersecurity and

Infrastructure Security Agency (CISA) is in the final stages of promulgating a rule, mandated by the Cyber Incident Reporting for Critical Infrastructure Act of 2022 (CIRCIA; P.L. 117-103), that will require a broad swath of businesses in 16 critical infrastructure sectors to file reports on major cybersecurity incidents within 72 hours; such reports to CISA are currently voluntary. The CIRCIA data collection stands to play a considerable role in information collection related to the cybercrime of ransomware, requiring that ransomware payments be reported within 24 hours. The exact list of categories for incidents reportable under CIRCIA is still under development—in late September 2024, CISA issued a draft set of revisions to its standard incident report that borrows Actions and other coding structures from VERIS.

A new rule by the Securities and Exchange Commission (SEC; 88 F.R. 51896) recently took effect as well, obliging publicly traded companies to disclose major cybersecurity incidents (many of which may constitute cybercrime) within four business days of being deemed a material threat. Thus, while individual CIRCIA reports are meant to be kept confidential by CISA, transparency for the investor public is the driving purpose of the SEC rule.

International Parallels: Cybercrime Data Collection in Canada and the Cyber Classification Compendium

The Canadian UCR Program, administered by a branch of Statistics Canada, shares its acronym with its U.S. counterpart but differs in other respects; police-report statistics are mandatory in Canada, not voluntary, and are commonly extracted directly from the police records management systems (RMS) used by local agencies. Beginning in 2004, the UCR Survey added a two-part Cyber Crime variable to the collection, with both parts premised on the definition of whether a computer (later generalized to refer to information and communication technology broadly) was the target of the offense or the instrument used to commit the offense. The first question asked for a yes/no response as to whether the offense was cybercrime under this definition, and the second question asked which type (i.e., target or instrument) applied. In 2024, the UCR Survey began collecting information using a new classification scheme, expanding the cybercrime type question to include nine response categories—Malware; System and Service Availability; Information Gathering; Intrusion; Data Release (information security compromise); Frauds; Abusive Content; Exploitation, Harassment, or Abuse of a Person; and Uncategorized—drawn from the main headings used in the Cyber Classification Compendium, which is an attempt to create a crosswalk between cybercrime offense types and definitions in international and U.S. law (Wright & Parker, 2023). Because full implementation of the new variable began only recently, its effectiveness remains unknown.

DEVELOPING A TAXONOMY OF CYBERCRIME

In our review of the partitioning and classification of cybercrime, we observed numerous dimensions along which cybercrime offenses might be structured. Notably, these include the degree of cyber/computer involvement and the role of the computer in the offense. Efforts to distill sets of fundamental nature-of-harm groups are also common.

We also reviewed the handling of cybercrime in all-crime taxonomies—notably our predecessor MNCS panel's classification of crime (National Academies, 2016a) and the International Classification of Crime for Statistical Purposes (United Nations Office on Drugs and Crime, 2015) on which that classification was based. Both systems define a set of fundamental cyber-specific nature-of-harm categories—unlawful access, unlawful interference, unlawful interception/access of data, and other—to characterize pure cyber-dependent crimes. But both systems rely on coding a base offense and toggling a cybercrime-involvement indicator to construct the vast bulk of cyber-enabled crimes—for instance, extortion plus the cybercrime indicator to connote ransomware or use of the cybercrime indicator to flag computer-related sexual exploitation offenses.

As the MNCS panel did in its reports, we established a set of principles and desired characteristics for our own recommended taxonomy. We sought a taxonomy satisfying all the requirements of a classification for statistical purposes, meaning we aimed to make it exhaustive of all cybercrime, partition it into mutually exclusive categories, and follow a hierarchical structure to the extent possible. We also sought a taxonomy with a small number of main categories, emphasizing the behavior that constitutes an offense without delving into technical jargon or fine-grained categories that may prove unworkable in law enforcement agencies' RMS specifications. We also sought definitions in the proposed taxonomy that were consistent with but not strictly limited by federal and state law, but also consistent with definitions in existing major collections.

Based on all the preceding, the taxonomy we recommend for cybercrime is given in short form below, expressed graphically in Figure S-1, and articulated in fuller detail in Appendix B.

> **Recommendation 3-1:** The following concise taxonomy should be used as an initial framework for developing statistical measures of cybercrime in the United States:
> 1 Acts Targeted Against Machines, Data, or Systems
>   1A Ransomware
>   1B Unlawful Access or Deprivation of Access
>   1C Unlawful Interference, Tampering, or Content Release
>   1D Other Acts Targeted Against Machines, Data, or Systems

    2 Fraud and Acts Targeted Against Property
       2A   Identity Theft
       2B   Fraud
       2C   Other Acts Targeted Against Property
    3 Acts Against Individuals, Nonsexual in Nature
    4 Acts Against Individuals, Sexual in Nature
    5 Acts Targeted Against Groups
    6 Acts Involving Incidental Technology Use
NA Acts with No Cyber/Computer Involvement

    Our recommended taxonomy is designed to be exhaustive of the degree of cyber/computer involvement, with main category 1 being pure cyber-dependent crime, categories 2–5 representing moderate levels of cyber-enabling of base crimes, and category 6 representing only cyber/computer involvement (with the final category of no cyber involvement completing the partitioning). Categories 2–5 are structured by the target of the offense, whether property, individual persons, or groups of people. Within major categories 1 and 2, we sparingly delineate specific named offenses, isolating ransomware due to its prominence in public discussion and retaining identity theft for continuity with existing NIBRS and NCVS Identity Theft Supplement usage.

    We intend our recommended taxonomy to be actionable and implementable with or without major revision of the underlying classification used for all crime, in the NIBRS or other systems. We concur with the MNCS panel that the nation's current crime statistics fall short of capturing information on new, important, and emerging types of crime, and we support the aspirational goal of a next-generation NIBRS that can cover a wider array of offense types. Presently, however, we recognize the uniquely delicate and challenging climate for crime and cybercrime data collection, with the NIBRS still contending with the challenges of full implementation, the NCVS beginning to field comprehensively redesigned instruments, and the wide-sweeping mandatory CIRCIA reporting still awaiting issuance of the final rule. Accordingly, our suggestion is to use the recommended taxonomy as an enhanced attribute flag for incidents; in this way, it can add useful information to the NIBRS Hacking/Computer Invasion offense through the disaggregation provided by our category 1, and it can combine with other base offense codes in the NIBRS to cover many cyber-enabled crimes—all without the need for a prior major revamping of code lists.

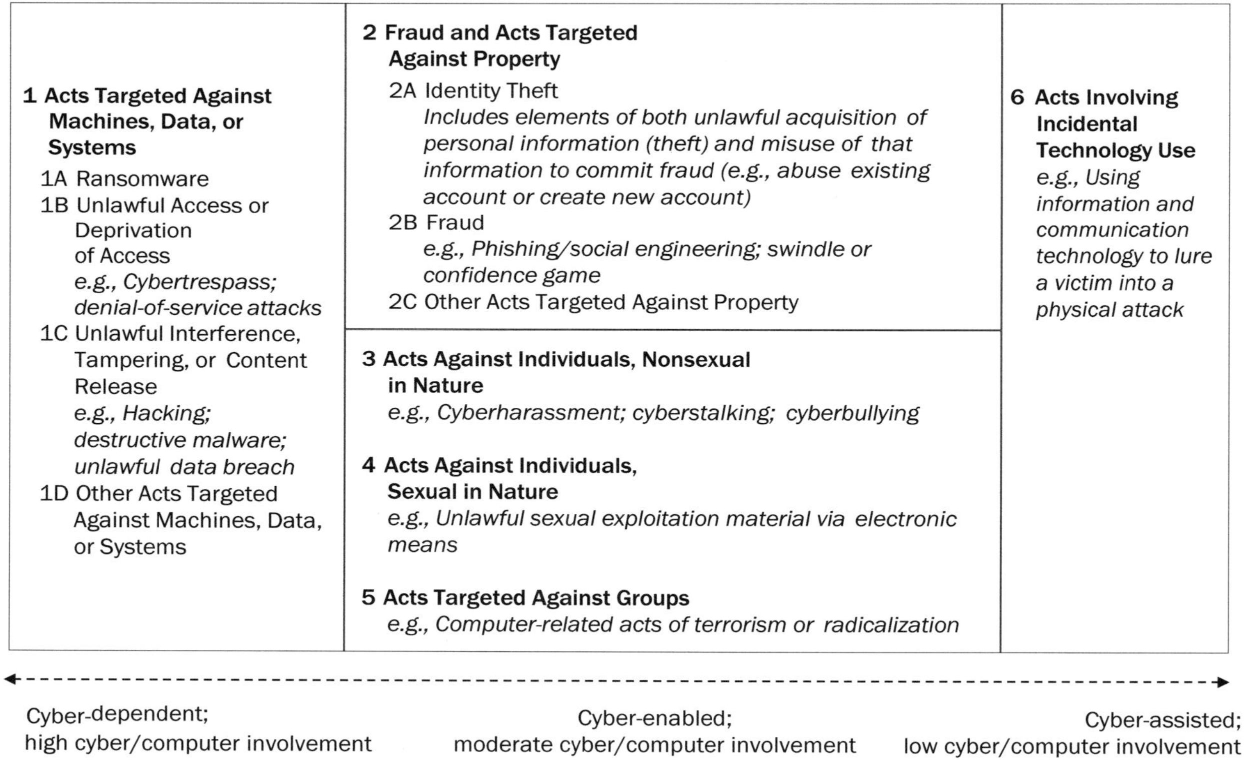

1 Acts Targeted Against Machines, Data, or Systems

1A Ransomware
1B Unlawful Access or Deprivation of Access
  e.g., Cybertrespass; denial-of-service attacks
1C Unlawful Interference, Tampering, or Content Release
  e.g., Hacking; destructive malware; unlawful data breach
1D Other Acts Targeted Against Machines, Data, or Systems

2 Fraud and Acts Targeted Against Property

2A Identity Theft
  Includes elements of both unlawful acquisition of personal information (theft) and misuse of that information to commit fraud (e.g., abuse existing account or create new account)
2B Fraud
  e.g., Phishing/social engineering; swindle or confidence game
2C Other Acts Targeted Against Property

3 Acts Against Individuals, Nonsexual in Nature
  e.g., Cyberharassment; cyberstalking; cyberbullying

4 Acts Against Individuals, Sexual in Nature
  e.g., Unlawful sexual exploitation material via electronic means

5 Acts Targeted Against Groups
  e.g., Computer-related acts of terrorism or radicalization

6 Acts Involving Incidental Technology Use
  e.g., Using information and communication technology to lure a victim into a physical attack

Cyber-dependent; high cyber/computer involvement ⟵⟶ Cyber-enabled; moderate cyber/computer involvement ⟵⟶ Cyber-assisted; low cyber/computer involvement

FIGURE S-1 Schematic of proposed classification of cybercrime.
SOURCE: Panel generated.

Recommendation 3-2: Rather than have a cybercrime classification function as parallel or adjunct to existing crime classifications, the taxonomy presented in Recommendation 3-1 should be implemented in crime data–collection systems as an attribute, flag, or modifier to code incidents in conjunction with the system's base classification of criminal offenses.

FURTHER RECOMMENDATIONS AND IMPLEMENTATION CHALLENGES

Calibrate Expectations: Cybercrime Estimation as a System-of-Systems

In the panel's opinion, improvements in cybercrime measurement are definitely possible, but it is important to approach such changes with tempered expectations. Cybercrime's breadth as a concept and its inherent mismatch with current data-collection practices means that adding a single category to an RMS or a single question to a survey will not suffice. Producing reliable estimates of cybercrime will necessitate a system-of-systems spanning multiple data sources, with each source collecting information on offenses and characteristics of offenses according to its unique strengths. An exact enumeration of cybercrime from any single data resource is unlikely.

Conclusion 4-1: Improving cybercrime measurement is important, but it is equally important that improvements be made with tempered, realistic expectations of the timing and extent of improvement. Cybercrime is an expansive and evolving topic, so it is unlikely that any single statistical source will effectively cover all of its dimensions; analysts will need to make best use of available information from an array of sources to derive markers of cybercrime activity.

Measuring Cybercrime by Leveraging Existing Data-Collection Efforts

Recommendations for the National Incident-Based Reporting System

While we support expansion of NIBRS's content coverage, we also observe that improved cybercrime collection in the NIBRS is critically dependent on clarification of purpose and intent. Simply adding categories or variables to the NIBRS would be for naught in the absence of clear guidance on how cybercrime is meant to be reported in that system—if individuals or businesses are to be encouraged to report cybercrime incidents to SLTT law enforcement agencies as a matter of good practice and if SLTT agencies, in turn, are to be encouraged to report them in the NIBRS. Accordingly, in the near term, we recommend a series of actions to take stock of NIBRS's current cybercrime-related content and establish the conditions for successful implementation of the recommended taxonomy.

> Recommendation 4-1: The Federal Bureau of Investigation Uniform Crime Reporting Program should consider the following modifications to the existing National Incident-Based Reporting System (NIBRS), preparatory to a more comprehensive cybercrime-collection effort:
> 1. Continue collecting the existing NIBRS offense categories of Hacking/Computer Invasion and Identity Theft, while actively encouraging participating law enforcement agencies to report these offenses;
> 2. Clarify the definition and intended role of the two NIBRS data elements that nominally indicate cybercrime involvement, Data Element 8 with Computer Equipment as response to Offender Suspected of Using and Data Element 9 with Cyberspace as response to Location;
> 3. Consider adding data/systems and digital currency/cryptocurrency as additional intangible property types in Data Element 14 (Type Property Loss/Etc.); and
> 4. Work with the records management system vendor community to ease NIBRS data entry and improve understanding of new elements, and incorporate information and examples associated with these modifications as part of NIBRS data-provider education and training.

This guidance acknowledges that the initial cybercrime categories added to the NIBRS—Hacking/Computer Invasion and Identity Theft—were a reasonable starting position. Hence, rather than requiring that these initial cybercrime categories be fundamentally overhauled up front, we suggest that the intent and objectives of the categories be clarified, and their collection bolstered and promoted as a norm for the NIBRS. Finally, the near-term guidance speaks to the importance of working with RMS vendors; we concur with the MNCS panel that data systems like the NIBRS will be most effective when data submissions are a routine by-product of agencies' day-to-day use of their own RMS rather than a separate reporting task.

These near-term, preparatory suggestions are meant to ease the way for more fundamental change.

> Recommendation 4-2: Following the preparatory steps of Recommendation 4-1, and possibly in conjunction with adoption of a modern classification of crime for statistical purposes, the Federal Bureau of Investigation should incorporate the cybercrime taxonomy in Recommendation 3-1 as a new, mandatory data element in the National

Incident-Based Reporting System Incident Segment. Implementing this new data element may involve consolidating or revising existing computer/cyber-related responses in Data Elements 8 and 9.

Recommendations for the National Crime Victimization Survey and Its Supplements

With respect to the NCVS, our guidance is similar if more pointed in terms of long-term work. The NCVS's nature as a household survey makes it uniquely suited to generate contextual information about crimes and cybercrimes with a distinctly personal effect. Importantly, the NCVS can suggest explanations about why incidents may not be reported to SLTT law enforcement or other authorities. We suggest that additional periodic supplements to the NCVS could effectively address personal-impact cybercrimes such as phishing/social engineering (as a variant of fraud) and image-based sexual abuse (including cyber-enabled sextortion).

Recommendation 4-3: The Bureau of Justice Statistics should leverage its existing National Crime Victimization Survey supplements with cybercrime-related content (Supplemental Fraud Survey, Identity Theft Supplement, Supplemental Victimization Survey) to contribute to the nation's understanding of cybercrime. This includes refining the content of those supplements as needed as well as working with data users to facilitate analysis and use of the resulting data, including comparison with other data sources.

Recommendation 4-4: Pending the availability of additional resources for victimization survey work, the Bureau of Justice Statistics should consider increasing the frequency of the three existing cybercrime-related supplements or the fielding of a dedicated cybercrime supplement.

To be very clear on this point, we do not recommend adding cybercrime-related content to the core NCVS, neither as a permanent part of the NCVS-1 Basic Screen Questionnaire nor to the detailed NCVS-2 Crime Incident Report completed for each victimization incident identified in the screener. We believe that the supplemental module approach is better suited for cybercrime-related content than revisions to core NCVS content.

Other Data-Collection Systems

While we do not offer specific targeted recommendations for other data-collection systems beyond the NIBRS and the NCVS, such systems are potentially part of the system-of-systems approach mentioned previously, and thus we encourage their development and eventual role in comprehensive cybercrime measurement. As the CIRCIA collection nears deployment of a final rule and begins mandatory data collection, it is important to both encourage and evaluate this collection for its potential to provide useful cybercrime information, particularly regarding ransomware; new SEC cybersecurity incident reporting rules warrant similar attention and assessment. Furthermore, as Statistics Canada begins to encourage constituent law enforcement agencies to report data using a detailed list of cybercrime codes, this work should be examined to apply lessons to U.S. NIBRS collection and training.

Aspirational Goals for Cybercrime Measurement

Governance and Coordination of National Cybercrime Statistics

Addressing the lack of an overall governance and coordination structure for crime statistics is a pressing need. Currently, no entity is directly tasked with drawing inference from multiple sources of crime data, and such a structure is arguably even more critical for cybercrime, given the array of public- and private-sector players at work in the field. Thus, we advocate for the creation of an information clearinghouse for cybercrime data.

> *Conclusion 4-2: As is true of crime statistics in general, the thorough and effective measurement of cybercrime and cyber-enabled crime will remain largely unobtainable absent the development of a governance and coordina-ion process for the collection of cybercrime reports and statistics. Cybercrime measurement is sufficiently fragmented that it is in particularly acute need of an information clearinghouse apparatus, meaning the designation of a specific party or parties to compile the various cybercrime measures that are and will be available and analyze common findings and trends.*

It is vitally important that these coordination, governance, and information clearinghouse functions provide overall direction to the cybercrime measurement enterprise. This includes analyzing the full range of public and private data and assessing strengths and weaknesses therein to produce the highest-quality estimates. Additionally, it involves articulating basic rules to ensure accurate data collection (e.g., counting rules for handling multivictim incidents) as well as clarifying the ideal avenue for cybercrime reporting by individuals (i.e., it may be judged most efficient for individuals to report to the IC3 and rely on the IC3 to report data to the NIBRS).

While we note the current absence of information clearinghouse structures and reinforce the need for them, we did not designate specific entities, although the U.S. Office of Management and Budget may be ideally positioned to broker and structure necessary discussions across federal agencies (National Academies, 2018, Recommendation 3.1). The information clearinghouse function for cybercrime may fit within the legally defined mission of the BJS or the stated mission of the IC3 but might also fit into some adaptation of Verizon's work coordinating cybercrime input from government and industry partners. One reason for declining to formally recommend an entity to perform the coordination and governance functions is that we do not think it appropriate to create the appearance of a major unfunded mandate on any particular agency or organization.

An essential task of any clearinghouse function will be the periodic revision and refinement of applicable definitions, including our recommended taxonomy—the taxonomy we propose is not a static document but rather an initial effort. New category breaks may be suggested by reported data; and taxonomy categories, codes, and examples necessitate periodic review to ensure inclusivity of new/emerging technologies.

Businesses and Organizations as Actors in Crime and Cybercrime Data Collection

Successful cybercrime measurement will rely on the increased and continuing participation of businesses and organizations in reporting cybercrime incidents—a difficult task due to both reluctance of businesses to appear vulnerable and complex liability issues that may arise for some business sectors.

To improve future cybercrime measurement, it will be important to monitor development of the CIRCIA and SEC mandatory-report systems for registering major cybersecurity incidents. Ideally, the CIRCIA collection—with its broad sweep and detailed focus on ransomware incidents—could evolve into a statistical data collection, with resulting data illustrating sector-wise trends and informing responses and interventions to cybercrime attacks. Additionally, major information-sharing vehicles (e.g., the Verizon DBIR series, ISACs and ISAOs, and the NCFTA) could add unique context and empirical insights that could aid the generation of reliable, consistent statistics while helping business effectively navigate the current cyberthreat landscape.

Finally, we propose that a commercial victimization survey may help to provide similar valuable contextual information about offenses not reported to authorities (and the reasons for not reporting) as the NCVS adds to the UCR/NIBRS in the national crime statistics conversation. A survey of businesses' victimization experiences was part of the original National Crime Survey program, but it was discontinued. The BJS also conducted a

National Computer Security Survey in 2006, but that has not been repeated. General improvements in conducting establishment surveys and, perhaps, increased interest in crime committed against businesses and organizations of all sizes suggest that timing may be ideal to revisit the idea of a commercial victimization survey, with cybercrime as an important component.

> **Recommendation 4-5: Pending the availability of resources to do so, the Bureau of Justice Statistics and federal agency partners should consider conducting additional rounds of the 2006 National Computer Security Survey, or otherwise field an establishment crime/cybercrime victimization survey, to collect data on crime/cybercrime victimization experiences by businesses and organizations. Such efforts should build on improvements in the conduct of establishment surveys and serve as a complementary marker of cybercrime that is not reported to authorities.**

Exploring the Cybercrime and Cybersecurity Nexus

As cybercrime data collection continues and evolves, ideally building from the conceptual base suggested in our recommended taxonomy, it will be important to address the "cyber" part of cybercrime as well as the "crime" component. Metrics in the cybersecurity realm, such as the nature and volume of detected-but-deflected attempts to bring down network resources or analyses of specific technological vectors along which cyberattacks are conducted, may better inform future cybercrime metrics, just as studies of policing, community resilience, and deterrence enhance understanding of crime.

1

Introduction: Cybercrime Measurement, the Panel, and Its Charge

Cybercrime poses serious threats and financial costs to individuals and businesses in the United States and worldwide. Reports of data breaches and ransomware attacks on governments and businesses have become common, as have incidents against individuals including identity theft and online stalking and harassment. Concern over cybercrime has increased as the internet has become a ubiquitous part of modern life. However, comprehensive, consistent, and reliable data and metrics on cybercrime still do not exist—a paucity of vital information that undoubtedly results from the exceedingly decentralized nature of relevant data collection at the national level. The U.S. Government Accountability Office (2023; USGAO) identified at least 13 federal agencies with some stake in collecting cybercrime-related data, which the USGAO grouped into three mechanisms governing the extent and nature of the data collection:[1]

- Agencies primarily tasked with the *identification* of cybercrime activity include the twin pillars of the U.S. national crime statistics apparatus, the Federal Bureau of Investigation's (FBI's) Uniform Crime Reporting (UCR) Program and the Bureau of Justice Statistics (BJS) (primarily through the National Crime Victimization Survey [NCVS] and its supplements), both within the U.S. Department of Justice (USDOJ). Other agencies sharing this identification function include the Cybersecurity & Infrastructure Security Agency in

---

[1] The U.S. Government Accountability Office (2023) report was mandated by the same Better Cybercrime Metrics Act that occasioned this panel's consensus study; see Appendix A.

the U.S. Department of Homeland Security, the Financial Crimes Enforcement Network in the U.S. Department of the Treasury, and the FBI's Internet Crime Complaint Center (IC3).
- Seven agencies collect data related to cybercrime during *investigation* of crime: the FBI (through its field offices); the Bureau of Alcohol, Tobacco, Firearms, and Explosives; and the Drug Enforcement Administration of the USDOJ, as well as the U.S. Secret Service and Homeland Security Investigations of the U.S. Department of Homeland Security, the Internal Revenue Service Criminal Investigation branch of the U.S. Department of the Treasury, and the U.S. Postal Inspection Service.
- Finally, the USDOJ as a whole is responsible for collecting and tracking certain relevant information related to cybercrime during the *prosecution* of cases.

The USGAO's overview of this data-collection terrain suggested wide variety in the manner and extent to which agencies collect or report data on cybercrime—and in the very capability of agencies' case management systems to categorize crimes as cyber-related or to track or identify cybercrime at all. Importantly, the USGAO review identified several fundamental challenges to cybercrime data collection. First, agencies lack a common, consistent definition of cybercrime, which necessarily complicates comparison across agencies. Second, the agencies act in isolation on their individual parts of the broader cybercrime problem; information is not collected or integrated by a single entity. Third, agencies consistently emphasized that cybercrime is almost certainly underreported—for a variety of reasons, the most blunt (as expressed in a USGAO interview with agency staff) being that victims necessarily "lack an incentive" to report cybercrime incidents "if it is not entirely clear who can do anything about it" (U.S. Government Accountability Office, 2023, p. 25).

Against this backdrop, two laws enacted in spring 2022 required the addition of cybercrime content in U.S. national crime statistics. In March 2022, provisions in the Violence Against Women Act (VAWA) Reauthorization Act of 2022 directed the FBI to "design and create [a] category for offenses that constitute cybercrimes against individuals" in the FBI UCR Program, which aggregates returns of offenses reported to state, local, tribal, and territorial (SLTT) law enforcement agencies. The VAWA Reauthorization Act language also required the FBI to "classify each type of cybercrime against individuals that is an offense under Federal or State law" as a reportable offense in the National Incident-Based Reporting System (NIBRS), the UCR Program's flagship database

(P.L. 117-103).[2] Two months later, the Better Cybercrime Metrics Act (BCMA; P.L. 117-116)[3] echoed the call for the FBI to "establish a category in the [NIBRS] for the collection of cybercrime and cyber-enabled crime reports" but also required that the BJS "include questions related to cybercrime victimization in the National Crime Victimization Survey [NCVS]," the household survey that serves as the dual major component of current U.S. national crime statistics through its ability to shed light on the extent of crime that is not reported to law enforcement. The BCMA further required that the FBI's revisions to the NIBRS expand the system's scope to cover "cybercrime and cyber-enabled crime faced by individuals and businesses" rather than just individuals—and it further required the FBI to commission this study to provide a basis for the revisions.

THE PANEL AND ITS CHARGE

As requested in the BCMA and sponsored by the FBI, the National Academies of Sciences, Engineering, and Medicine's (National Academies') Committee on National Statistics, Committee on Law and Justice, and Computer Science and Telecommunications Board convened this ad hoc consensus study panel (see Box 1-1).

The panel met in formal closed sessions five times over the course of the study and conducted additional deliberations in several virtual meetings. To inform its deliberations, the panel held several public sessions, at which invited experts shared their perspectives on cybercrime and current measurement and classification efforts. In the first public session, the panel heard from the study's sponsors at the FBI. During the second public session, the panel heard perspectives on conceptualizing cybercrime definitions, typologies, and taxonomies; perspectives on the measurement of identity theft; and perspectives from other models, such as the Canadian model for cybercrime data collection and the Cyber Classification Compendium. The panel also gathered insights from federal and state-level law enforcement and other federal agency efforts to capture cybercrime data, including the Cybersecurity & Infrastructure Security Agency, the IC3, the Federal Trade Commission, and the Michigan Cyber Command Center, and learned about the current collection of cybercrime-related data in the NIBRS and NCVS. Finally, the panel heard perspectives from interested constituencies, including the National Cyber-Forensics and Training

---

[2] See 136 Stat. 950 in particular; P.L. 117-103 is the sprawling omnibus appropriations act for fiscal year 2002 into which numerous other bills were folded, including both the VAWA Reauthorization Act and the Cyber Incident Reporting for Critical Infrastructure Act that is a major focus in this study.
[3] The full text of both the VAWA Reauthorization Act cybercrime reporting provisions and the BCMA is reprinted in Appendix A.

> **BOX 1-1**
> **Statement of Task**
>
> As requested in the Better Cybercrime Metrics Act, P.L. 117-116, the National Academies will convene an ad hoc committee to develop a taxonomy for the purpose of measuring different types of cybercrime, including both cyber-enabled and cyber-dependent crimes faced by individuals and businesses, and consider needs for its periodic revision. As part of its information gathering, the study will:
>
> 1. Consult with relevant stakeholders, including the Cybersecurity and Infrastructure Security Agency of the Department of Homeland Security; Federal, State, and local law enforcement agencies; and other government entities involved with the investigation or monitoring of cyber-enabled or cyber-dependent crimes; criminologists and academics; cybercrime and cybersecurity experts; victims of cybercrime; and business leaders and
> 2. Consider relevant taxonomies and metrics developed by non-governmental organizations, international organizations, academies, or other entities.
>
> The study report will provide conclusions and recommendations for a taxonomy that can be used by the Federal Bureau of Investigation and the Bureau of Justice Statistics to measure cyber-enabled and cyber-dependent crimes in the National Incident-Based Reporting System, the National Crime Victimization Survey, or any successor systems.

Alliance, the Association of State Uniform Crime Reporting Programs, the Identity Theft Resource Center, and AARP.

The panel also drew heavily on the work of the predecessor National Academies' Panel on Modernizing the Nation's Crime Statistics (hereafter, the MNCS panel), which was jointly sponsored by the BJS and the FBI and faced an even broader mandate than our panel: develop a taxonomy of all crime and advise on its implementation for improving U.S. crime statistics. The MNCS panel's first report (National Academies, 2016a) provided a detailed classification of crime for statistical purposes, expressly to include new and emerging crime types that had not been factored into U.S. crime statistics to date. With respect to cybercrime (and as we discuss in more detail in Chapter 3), the MNCS panel delineated some computer-specific offenses as a subcategory of crimes involving property but—more generally—called for the use of a cybercrime-involvement attribute flag to be coded alongside a base offense (e.g., extortion or fraud) to indicate "whether the use of computer data or computer systems was an integral part of the modus operandi of the offense" (National Academies, 2016a,

p. 136). This approach would permit, for example, examination of cyberharassment and cyberbullying as instances of the base offense of harassment plus the cybercrime-involvement flag, rather than as separate offense categories. In that first report, the MNCS panel noted that cybercrime is a "sufficiently broad and diverse concept that it could warrant a fully-realized three- or four-level hierarchical classification on its own" (National Academies, 2016a, p. 153) but argued for its simple, flexible approach rather than trying to craft a specific subcategory for every new cybercrime-related variant. In its second report (National Academies, 2018), the MNCS panel turned to issues of implementation, including the fit of the expansive recommended taxonomy with extant crime statistics data-collection systems and the perennial challenge of collecting data on offenses against both individuals and businesses—themes of clear and direct import to our own panel's task of improving cybercrime measurement. Both MNCS panel reports developed the theme that crime is too broad and varied a topic to be covered well by any single data-collection system and instead envisioned a national crime statistics system-of-systems, in which the traditional report-to-law-enforcement (i.e., NIBRS) and survey research (i.e., NCVS) approaches would be supplemented by new administrative-record-type data resources. As described in this report, we believe that the same approach applies with equal force to the broad terrain of cybercrime.

INTERPRETING THE CHARGE: THE CHALLENGES OF CLASSIFYING AND MEASURING CYBERCRIME

To carry out the statement of task, we were guided by several central precepts that underlie our approach to the study.

Definitional Issues: Crime, Cybercrime, Cybersecurity, and the Law

The first guiding precept is a direct extension of the clear focus on the fit of cybercrime and cyber-enabled crime within the existing national crime statistics apparatus, embodied in the VAWA Reauthorization Act, the BCMA, and the panel's statement of task. Put simply, we cast this study of cybercrime as crime-centric rather than cyber-centric; we interpreted the statement of task as obligating us to consider cybercrime as crime with a cyber/criminal component rather than cyberactivity with a criminal component. The MNCS panel adopted a compound definition of crime as "a class of socially unacceptable behavior that directly harms or threatens harm to others" but also—at root—as "that activity that is both unlawful and subject to certain punishments or sanctions" (National Academies, 2016a, pp. 21, 23). Thus, the offenses defined in its proposed classifications are behavioral in nature, but the definitions almost always include the word "unlawful," precisely to distinguish between bad or undesirable behavior and actual crime. This study followed the same approach. We adopted the MNCS panel's definition of crime as a basis and then defined "cybercrime" as crime in which computers, data, and networks—information and communication technology (ICT)—are central to commission of the offense.[4] This definition focuses attention on the offending behavior/actions rather than the specific technological mechanics by which the offenses are committed. Consequently, our definition focuses on harmful cyberactivity that is distinctly unlawful rather than merely undesirable; for instance, trolling (i.e., posting deliberately provocative or disruptive content on the internet with the intent of eliciting strong reactions from others) is not in itself a cybercrime, though it can be if it crosses the line into harassment or bullying.

Two important corollaries follow from this precept. Playing out the converse, this study would have been much different if it were cyber-centric in nature, focused on computer and technology use that could be considered crime. Accordingly, in this study, we did not weigh the adequacy of cybercrime content or coverage in federal and state law but rather used existing law as a guidepost to behaviors that are already interpretable as crime or cybercrime. That said, the rate of change in ICT—and the resultant potential for important new cybercrime variants to arise—is such that it will be important to reassess and update our recommended taxonomy over time. Another important corollary relates to which "law" is the standard by which cybercrime is deemed unlawful, which hearkens to a major challenge faced by the MNCS panel in considering matters such as environmental and white-collar crime. Generally speaking—and acknowledging that lines of distinction are not always sharp in crimes involving businesses and organizations—our panel's emphasis skews heavily toward criminal law and justice rather than civil justice or purely regulatory behaviors. On a practical level, we cannot and do not dwell on higher-level matters such as liability related to cybercrime and cybersecurity. For instance, the shape and extent of privacy legislation at the federal and state levels is an important societal issue but not directly germane to our task; we aimed to define a taxonomy that allows for measurement of when a (criminal) data breach occurs, but it was outside our direct task to weigh in on business or agency data-stewardship responsibilities or purely civil/regulatory sanctions that may arise for data holders when a breach occurs.

Relatedly, we note that cybercrime and cybersecurity (more precisely, cybersecurity incidents or breaches) are strongly related concepts, but they

---

[4] Fully expanded, this means that the panel defines cybercrime as that class of socially unacceptable activity for which ICT is central to the commission of the offense, that directly harms or threatens harm to others and is both unlawful and subject to certain punishment and sanctions.

are not equivalent. Many cybersecurity incidents, being conducted with malicious intent, are cybercrimes, but the association is not automatic. Data breaches or severely disruptive cybersecurity events can happen through simple error (e.g., human or technological/programming error) or as a direct consequence of environmental or physical factors. Hence, while there is strong overlap between the concepts and much to be learned about cybercrime-measurement practices from practices that measure cybersecurity in general, it is essential that the two are not automatically equated.

Ill Fit of Cybercrime with Existing National Crime Statistics Apparatus

A second major precept underlying our panel's approach to the problem of cybercrime classification and measurement is, again, a direct extension of the VAWA Reauthorization Act, the BCMA, and our statement of task, with their focus on the fit of cybercrime within the existing national crime statistics apparatus (i.e., NIBRS and NCVS). It is a simple point but one that we believe rises to the level of statement as a formal conclusion—it must be acknowledged that cybercrime is inherently difficult to fully square with that apparatus.

> *Conclusion 1-1: Measurement of cybercrime is challenging—particularly in the context of current U.S. national crime statistics—for a number of reasons, including expected underreporting, the variable scope and nature of incidents, and the changing nature of technology.*

Though the switch to the NIBRS has expanded the scope of crime coverage—and the reports of the MNCS panel (National Academies, 2016a, 2018) argue convincingly for a still-wider scope—U.S. crime statistics remain heavily geared toward the measurement of so-called street crime, meaning violent and interpersonal crime. Relative to the traditional crime types, cybercrime is difficult to conceptualize in current crime statistics because, depending on the definition and framing of the incident, the "cyber" component of cybercrime offenses could be characterized as the victim, offender, modus operandi, motive, location, or even the weapon used in the offense. The existing national crime statistics apparatus is primarily focused on person-level reporting, with accurate measurement of commercial, institutional, and organizational crime being a long-standing challenge—a difficulty for our work given the extent to which cybercrime is targeted at businesses and organizations.

As a further complication, cybercrime is subject to inherent, expected underreporting to SLTT law enforcement by individuals and businesses alike. Individuals may not report incidents of cybercrime simply because they may not be aware that they are the victim of a cybercrime (e.g., not knowing of inclusion in a data breach unless notified) or they may not find it natural or helpful to report to law enforcement (e.g., reporting credit card theft to the card issuer to gain immediate relief but not filing a report with local police). Businesses and organizations, meanwhile, may be reluctant to report cybercrime incidents to law enforcement, at least in part due to fear of reputational damage and commensurate competitive disadvantage. In addition, as discussed further in Chapter 2, businesses and organizations may already be obligated to report major cybersecurity incidents (many of which are cybercrimes) to various incident-report teams and cybersecurity entities, and reporting to local authorities may be considered superfluous. As the U.S. Government Accountability Office (2023, p. 25) report bore out, businesses and individuals alike may lack incentive to report cybercrime to relevant authorities due to the perception that local authorities are equipped neither to make restitution for losses nor to apprehend offenders, and thus there is nothing to be gained from filing a report. Furthermore, while some state and large-city law enforcement agencies may have dedicated cybercrime offices or teams that investigate criminal cyberincidents, that is not universally the case. Thus, individuals who do want to report, for example, an experience of computer-based consumer fraud to local law enforcement may be referred to the same support organizations and entities (e.g., Better Business Bureau or AARP) that may in turn suggest notifying local law enforcement—a cycle borne out of basic confusion over which cybercrime incidents should be reported and to whom.

As yet another complication, there are several long-standing challenges in measuring crime in current data-collection systems that may be especially problematic in focusing on cybercrime, several of which are raised in the MNCS panel's reports. These challenges may make the boundaries and basic parameters of cybercrime incidents difficult to determine or report.

- Cybercrimes that affect systems or networks are quintessential examples of what the MNCS panel described as nondenumerable crimes (National Academies, 2018, p. 32), for which it is difficult to generate a meaningful, accurate incident count or other metrics. Cybercrime attacks can have ripple effects, possibly beginning with one or a small number of target devices but ultimately swelling to affect (if not directly victimize) thousands or millions of downstream individuals. In the panel's view, it is difficult to say for certain how many offenses or how many victims should be counted to fairly represent a ransomware attack on a hospital, for example: the single machine(s) in which the attack was successful or the number of accounts or machines baited; the number of locked machines or potential users of those specific on-network but locked devices; or the broader pool of individuals suffering harm from the incident, such as people harmed by the inability to access medicine or treatment due to the ransomware lock. Likewise, a corporate data breach could expose millions of individuals to some chance of harm through identity theft; if all of these incidents are to be reported to law enforcement, the question is whether the resulting spike in local crime statistics would be a local, state, or federal responsibility. Likewise, even the number of suspected offenders in a cyberattack can be difficult to ascertain.

- The NIBRS and NCVS are intended to capture both completed and attempted offenses, although some crime types are logically more prone to having attempted-but-incomplete occurrences go unreported or even unnoticed by potential victims. Cybercrime measurement systems should likewise include both attempts and completions—for instance, the development of malicious software is commonly considered a crime in itself, regardless of whether the code is activated (or effective)—but cybercrime suggests additional complexities. For example, for the sake of tractability, it makes sense to treat a completed denial-of-service attack as a single incident, a barrage of illegitimate traffic that overwhelms a targeted system, yet that underlying single barrage may comprise thousands if not millions of disruptive requests/pings. But drawing a line between an attempted-but-unsuccessful denial-of-service attack and a (noncriminal) high-volume day may be difficult, leave aside measuring potential attacks that are actively blocked or prevented by cybersecurity measures.

- The single point-in-time nature of crime statistics data collection is a challenge for measuring many offense types; at the time that a crime becomes known to local law enforcement, little may be known about the offender, and those answers await further investigation (if they are available at all). This may be particularly vexing in the cybercrime context, where the full extent of actors involved in the perpetration may take weeks or months to determine. This timing issue may affect the determination of what label might apply to a cybercrime; for example, a single ransomware attack or an isolated denial-of-service attempt may be part of a broader Advanced Persistent Threat, a program of coordinated, sustained cyberattacks, and establishing connections between the events may require additional investigative time. It may be difficult to peg specific times related to incidents like the deployment of spyware, performing passive monitoring of the system; the time when the spyware is detected may be known, but it may take time to unravel how long the software was in place.

Finally, the evolving nature of technology results in continually evolving cybercrime types and nomenclature; managing that flux can be difficult when generating crime statistics. Such evolution fundamentally heightens the importance of a mechanism for occasional updating and revision of a cybercrime taxonomy. In Chapter 3, we argue that this rate of change is also a reason for a taxonomy to focus on a relatively small number of behavior-specific (vs. technology-specific) offenses rather than trying to carve out hyper-specific categories for every slight variant. We describe the general nature of federal and state cybercrime law in Appendix C and the specific nature of the NIBRS implementation in Chapter 2 but, in this overview, suffice it to say that the closest fit for some cybercrime offenses as currently defined in the NIBRS bears the name of an outdated communication technology (i.e., wire fraud); even references to computers and network involvement may fail to convey the sweep of computing technology (e.g., smartphones and social media platforms); and reconciling current cybercrime definitions with the capabilities of new and emerging technologies is a major looming problem. A closing precept, and one that shaped the panel's approach to this study, is that the heightened interest in measuring cybercrime comes at a critical juncture for both major planks of the existing national crime statistics apparatus into which we aim to craft a larger role for cybercrime. Though the FBI's UCR Program has been in operation since 1929 and the NIBRS has been in development for nearly 40 years, the NIBRS only became the program's flagship in January 2021, after the official retiring of the predecessor Summary Reporting System. The NIBRS is still in the early stages of near-full-scale implementation and still grappling with the challenge of ensuring that the nation's more than 18,000 law enforcement agencies comply with the new reporting standard. Meanwhile, the NCVS is presently in the midst of one of the cycles of major revision and reinvention that have been a hallmark of the survey's quality and success, while contending with the pervasive challenges of survey nonresponse and difficulties in conducting survey interviews. These developments—and corresponding developments in the general arena of cybersecurity reporting described in Chapter 2—all argue for caution regarding the extent of change that is feasible and realizable in these and other systems driving cybercrime measurement. This report focuses on both near-term objectives and longer-term, more aspirational objectives, in the hopes of preventing the perfect from being the enemy of the good.

ORGANIZATION OF THE REPORT

The analysis of cybercrime classification and measurement in this report unfolds in three major pieces. Chapter 2 discusses current data collections that touch on aspects of cybercrime, including the NIBRS and the NCVS.

In these synopses, we place particular attention on the offense code lists used in data-collection efforts. In Chapter 3, we turn to various approaches advanced for classifying cybercrime, both independently and in the context of all crime. We develop a set of principles and desired design features and, based on those, present a recommended taxonomy for cybercrime classification. Finally, Chapter 4 lays out the panel's recommendations for implementing the cybercrime taxonomy, including opportunities for leveraging existing data-collection efforts and aspirational goals for future cybercrime measurement.

Several appendices provide additional detail. Appendix A reprints both the 2022 cybercrime reporting visions in the VAWA Reauthorization Act and the BCMA. Appendix B is this panel's main deliverable—the recommended classification of cybercrime for statistical purposes, with definitions and specific inclusions in each category. Appendix C lists cybercrime offenses defined in current systems and law. Appendix D provides biographical sketches of panel members and principal staff.

2

Treatment of Cybercrime in Current Data Collections

In this chapter, we briefly review how cybercrime and related concepts are measured in existing and developing data systems, with particular eye to the categorization schemes used in those systems.

CYBERCRIME HANDLING IN THE NATIONAL INCIDENT-BASED REPORTING SYSTEM

The Uniform Crime Reporting (UCR) Program is a data series compiled and maintained by the Federal Bureau of Investigation (FBI) based on the voluntary data contributions of thousands of state, local, tribal, and territorial (SLTT) law enforcement agencies.[1] The program began in 1929

---

[1]Because it is directly quoted in the Better Cybercrime Metrics Act (see Appendix A) and because it is germane to the panel's task, an important exception to the UCR Program's voluntary reporting structure deserves notice. The Uniform Federal Crime Reporting Act of 1988 (P.L. 115-393; 102 Stat. 4468; 34 U.S.C. § 41303) requires "all departments and agencies within the Federal government (including the Department of Defense) which routinely investigate complaints of criminal activity" to report crimes in their jurisdictions as part of the UCR Program, "limited to the reporting of those crimes comprising the Uniform Crime Reports." However, it would be 27 years (and a concerted effort to get some federal law enforcement agencies, including the FBI itself, to report) before UCR results for federal agencies were reported in the UCR Program's Crime in the United States report. Even the 2023 "Federal Tables" of Crime in the United States (accessible from the FBI's Crime Data Explorer at https://cde.ucr.cjis.gov/LATEST/webapp/#/pages/downloads) include submissions from 41 federal agencies (most being Offices of Inspector General, and not including the Bureau of Indian Affairs, which is tabulated separately) and are limited to the major violent and property crimes of the old Summary Reporting System described in this paragraph and in Box 2-1.

BOX 2-1
Crime Classification in the Uniform Crime Reporting Summary Reporting System, 2014

Part I Classes
1. Criminal homicide
   - 1a Murder and nonnegligent manslaughter
   - 1b Manslaughter by negligence
2. Rape
   - 2a Rape
   - 2b Attempts to commit rape
   - 2c Historical rape
3. Robbery
   - 3a Firearm
   - 3b Knife or cutting instrument
   - 3c Other dangerous weapon
   - 3d Strong-arm—hands, fists, feet, etc.
4. Aggravated assault
   - 4a Firearm
   - 4b Knife or cutting instrument
   - 4c Other dangerous weapon
   - 4d Strong-arm—hands, fists, feet, etc.—aggravated injury
5. Burglary
   - 5a Forcible entry
   - 5b Unlawful entry—no force
   - 5c Attempted forcible entry
6. Larceny—theft (except motor vehicle theft)
   - 6Xa Pocket-picking
   - 6Xb Purse-snatching
   - 6Xc Shoplifting
   - 6Xd Thefts from motor vehicles
   - 6Xe Theft of motor vehicle parts and accessories
   - 6Xf Theft of bicycles
   - 6Xg Theft from buildings
   - 6Xh Theft from coin-operated device or machine
   - 6Xi All other
7. Motor vehicle theft
   - 7a Autos
   - 7b Trucks and buses
   - 7c Other vehicles
8. Arson
   - Structural (Codes 8a–g cover different types of structures)
   - Mobile (Codes 8h–i differentiate between motor vehicles and other mobile property)
   - Other (Code 8j)

A. Human trafficking—commercial sex acts
B. Human trafficking—involuntary servitude

Part II Classes
9   Other assaults—simple, not aggravated (also codes 4e "as a quality control matter and for the purpose of looking at total assault violence")
10 Forgery and counterfeiting
11 Fraud
12 Embezzlement
13 Stolen property: buying, receiving, possessing
14 Vandalism
15 Weapons; carrying, possessing, etc.
16 Prostitution and commercialized vice
    16a Prostitution
    16b Assisting or promoting prostitution (also coded 30)
    16c Purchasing prostitution (also coded 31)
17 Sex offenses (except rape and prostitution and commercialized vice)
18 Drug abuse violations
19 Gambling
20 Offenses against the family and children
21 Driving under the influence
22 Liquor laws
23 Drunkenness
24 Disorderly conduct
25 Vagrancy
26 All other offenses
27 Suspicion
28 Curfew and loitering laws (persons under 18)
29 Runaways (persons under 18)

SOURCE: Reprinted from National Academies (2016a, Box 2.1), in turn excerpted from Federal Bureau of Investigation (2013b).

after the completion of a standard manual for UCR data collection by the International Association of Chiefs of Police. For decades, the centerpiece of the UCR Program was the Summary Reporting System (SRS), which—as the name implies—required the compilation of summary counts of offenses known (reported) to law enforcement agencies as well as arrest totals for seven major crime types dubbed Part I offenses. These seven Part I offenses (i.e., murder, rape, robbery, aggravated assault, burglary, larceny-theft, and motor vehicle theft) were selected both because of their perceived severity and their supposed consistency in definition across U.S. states; in later years, arson and human trafficking were added to Part I by law. Meanwhile, only arrest counts were collected for several other offenses, dubbed Part II crimes and generally interpreted as less severe offenses. "False personation, pretense, statement, document, representation, claims, evidence, etc." and "fraudulent use of telegraph, telephone messages"—predecessors of the eventual offenses of identity theft and wire fraud—were both listed as examples of the Part II offense of "embezzlement and fraud" in the original International Association of Chiefs of Police (1929, p. 28) manual that defined the UCR Program.

Part I and Part II SRS offenses, as they stood in 2014, are listed in Box 2-1. The hallmark characteristic of the SRS was its rigid adherence to a Hierarchy Rule—hierarchy in the sense of compression of information rather than rolling up (or down) to different levels of granularity in measurement. Under the SRS Hierarchy Rule, only the most serious offense in a crime incident was to be reported—homicide being the most serious, and continuing in the order listed in Box 2-1. So, for instance, only the homicide would be counted in an incident involving both homicide and motor vehicle theft. Moreover, popular attention was drawn principally to Part I offenses in determining whether crime rates were rising and falling; the arrest-only Part II offenses were given substantially less visibility.

After a task force issued recommendations for future development of the UCR Program in 1985 (Poggio et al., 1985), work began on what would become the National Incident-Based Reporting System (NIBRS), with a few pioneer law enforcement agencies beginning to submit data in the new format by the late 1980s.[2] The NIBRS eliminated the SRS Hierarchy Rule; all offenses (up to 10) committed as part of a single crime incident are meant to be included in a NIBRS data record. NIBRS data records for each incident grew to include nearly 60 data elements across six segments, providing a

---

[2] The task force on options for the future of the UCR Program was convened by the Bureau of Justice Statistics (BJS), an early moment in a continuing partnership between the BJS and the FBI. More recently, the BJS's grantmaking authority was essential to the multiyear National Crime Statistics Exchange program that worked to boost reporting to the FBI's UCR Program in NIBRS format prior to 2021.

wealth of information about each incident. The six segments of a NIBRS data record are as follows: Administrative (e.g., date and time of incident and identity of reporting law enforcement agency), Offense (e.g., offense type, method, and location), Property (e.g., type and value of property involved in the crime), Victim (e.g., demographic information and nature of relationship to offender), Offender, and Arrestee (if applicable).

Importantly, the NIBRS format permitted not only reporting of multiple offenses per incident but also a much wider variety of offense categories (see Table 2-1). The current NIBRS includes 71 specific Group A offenses under 28 categories, for which the full incident detail is meant to be reported; 10 Group B offenses are, like the predecessor SRS Part II, subject only to arrest-count reporting (Federal Bureau of Investigation, 2023b, pp. 16, 42). As depicted in Table 2-1, Group A offenses are also loosely grouped into three overarching categories, depending on whether the offense is deemed a crime against a person, against property, or against society.

Uptake of the new, detailed NIBRS reporting required substantial time and resources, and thus proceeded at a markedly slower rate than initially projected. Though NIBRS-format data were available to and analyzed by some researchers, those data were ultimately a self-selected sample of law enforcement agencies and not statistically representative of any broader population; the UCR Program itself did not publish a report of tabulations from NIBRS data until 2013. However, after 30 years of coexistence—the SRS continuing to be the official UCR format while law enforcement agencies were encouraged to invest resources in making the technological upgrade to the NIBRS format—the FBI officially discontinued the SRS as of January 1, 2021. Not all law enforcement agencies made the transition in time; as shown in Table 2-2, about 34 percent of federal and SLTT law enforcement agencies did not submit NIBRS-format data in 2021 and 2022, notably including the nation's two largest local law enforcement agencies, the New York Police Department and the Los Angeles Police Department (U.S. Department of Justice, 2023, p. 8). Most law enforcement agencies in five populous states—California, New York, Illinois, Pennsylvania, and Florida—did not report to NIBRS in 2021; NIBRS coverage in those states improved in 2022, though Florida and Pennsylvania remained at 7.7 and 9.1 percent agency participation, respectively.[3] Accordingly, the FBI's UCR Program continues to work on increasing full NIBRS participation.

Prior to 2021, cybercrime could only (at best) enter UCR figures if it was characterized as either a type of fraud or as "all other offenses"—both Part II entries in the SRS hierarchy, thus as an arrests-only count rather

---

[3] See https://www.themarshallproject.org/2022/06/14/what-did-fbi-data-say-about-crime-in-2021-it-s-too-unreliable-to-tell and https://www.themarshallproject.org/2023/07/13/fbi-crime-rates-data-gap-nibrs

TABLE 2-1 National Incident-Based Reporting System Offense Codes

NIBRS Code	Offense Name	Eligible for Location 58 Cyberspace	Crime Against
09A	Murder and Nonnegligent Manslaughter		Person
09B	Negligent Manslaughter		Person
09C	Justifiable Homicide		Not a Crime
11A	Rape		Person
11B	Sodomy[a]		Person
11C	Sexual Assault With An Object[a]		Person
11D	Fondling		Person
13A	Aggravated Assault		Person
13B	Simple Assault		Person
13C	Intimidation	Y	Person
23A	Pocket-picking		Property
23B	Purse-snatching		Property
23C	Shoplifting		Property
23D	Theft From Building		Property
23E	Theft From Coin-Operated Machine or Device		Property
23F	Theft From Motor Vehicle		Property
23G	Theft of Motor Vehicle Parts or Accessories		Property
23H	All Other Larceny		Property
26A	False Pretenses/Swindle/Confidence Game	Y	Property
26B	Credit Card/Automated Teller Machine Fraud	Y	Property
26C	Impersonation	Y	Property
26D	Welfare Fraud	Y	Property
26E	Wire Fraud	Y	Property
26F	Identity Theft	Y	Property
26G	Hacking/Computer Invasion	Y	Property
26H	Money Laundering[a]	Y	Society
30A	Illegal Entry into the United States[b]		Society
30B	False Citizenship[b]		Society
30C	Smuggling Aliens[b]		Society
30D	Re-entry after Deportation[b]		Society
35A	Drug/Narcotic Violations	Y	Society
35B	Drug Equipment Violations	Y	Society

continued

TABLE 2-1 Continued

NIBRS Code	Offense Name	Eligible for Location 58 Cyberspace	Crime Against
36A	Incest		Person
36B	Statutory Rape		Person
39A	Betting/Wagering	Y	Society
39B	Operating/Promoting/Assisting Gambling	Y	Society
39C	Gambling Equipment Violations	Y	Society
39D	Sports Tampering		Society
40A	Prostitution	Y	Society
40B	Assisting or Promoting Prostitution	Y	Society
40C	Purchasing Prostitution	Y	Society
49A	Harboring Escapee/Concealing from Arrest[b]		Society
49B	Flight to Avoid Prosecution[b]		Society
49C	Flight to Avoid Deportation[b]		Society
58A	Import Violations[b]		Society
58B	Export Violations[b]		Society
61A	Federal Liquor Offenses[b]		Society
61B	Federal Tabacco Offenses[b]		Society
64A	Human Trafficking, Commercial Sex Acts	Y	Person
64B	Human Trafficking, Involuntary Servitude	Y	Person
100	Kidnapping/Abduction		Person
101	Treason[b]	Y	Society
103	Espionage[b]	Y	Society
120	Robbery		Property
200	Arson		Property
210	Extortion/Blackmail	Y	Property
220	Burglary/Breaking and Entering		Property
240	Motor Vehicle Theft		Property
250	Counterfeiting/Forgery	Y	Property
270	Embezzlement	Y	Property
280	Stolen Property Offenses	Y	Property
290	Destruction/Damage/Vandalism of Property	Y	Property
360	Failure to Register as a Sex Offender[b]		Society
390	Pornography/Obscene Material	Y	Society

continued

TABLE 2-1 Continued

NIBRS Code	Offense Name	Eligible for Location 58 Cyberspace	Crime Against
510	Bribery	Y	Property
520	Weapon Law Violations	Y	Society
521	Violation of National Firearms Act of 1934[b]	Y	Society
522	Weapons of Mass Destruction[b]		Society
526	Explosives[b]	Y	Society
620	Wildlife Trafficking[b]		Society
720	Animal Cruelty		Society
90B	Curfew/Loitering/Vagrancy Violations		
90C	Disorderly Conduct		
90D	Driving Under the Influence		
90F	Family Offenses, Nonviolent		
90G	Liquor Law Violations		
90J	Trespass of Real Property		
90K	Failure to Appear[b]		
90L	Federal Resource Violations[b]		
90M	Perjury[b]		
90Z	All Other Offenses		

[a]Currently recoded to 11A but slated to be rejected as valid code in 2025.
[b]Offenses eligible for reporting by federal and tribal law enforcement agencies only.
SOURCES: Federal Bureau of Investigation (2023b); panel added column on cyberspace location eligibility based on Federal Bureau of Investigation (2023a, p. 52).

than a measure of offenses known to police. From the outset, then, the NIBRS has markedly increased the capacity for reporting cybercrime. In Appendix C, we trace the NIBRS handling of cybercrime-related concepts through various revisions of the system's user manual, briefly summarized in the following points.

In terms of defined crime categories, the NIBRS's long-standing guidance was to code computer crime offenses as the closest substantive offense—for instance, as fraud or embezzlement. By 2013, the offense of Wire Fraud was redefined in the NIBRS to include the use of computers and electronic messaging to perpetrate fraud. In 2014, the FBI director approved the addition of Hacking/Computer Invasion and Identity Theft as Group A offenses in the NIBRS, specifically to improve coverage of cybercrime. Both offenses fall under the general heading of crimes against

TABLE 2-2 Participation in National Incident-Based Reporting System by Law Enforcement Agencies, 2021–2022

	2021			2022		
	Submitted NIBRS Data	Total Agencies	Percentage of Agency Participation	Submitted NIBRS Data	Total Agencies	Percentage of Agency Participation
State and Local Agencies	12,523	18,746	66.8	12,515	18,678	67.0
Tribal Agencies	178	212	84.0	172	214	80.4
Federal Agencies	41	99	41.4	38	99	38.4
U.S. Territories	1	5	20.0	1	5	20.0
All Agencies	12,742	19,203	66.4	12,725	19,139	66.5

NOTES: The source report estimates that 73 percent of the U.S. population is represented by the 12,725 agencies that submitted National Incident-Based Reporting System (NIBRS) data in 2022. The number of agencies can decrease from year to year if the agency enters "covered" status, meaning that another agency assumes responsibility for reporting crime data for it, or it becomes dormant.
SOURCE: U.S. Department of Justice (2023, pp. 7–8).

property and bear code numbers designating them as variants of fraud. Though Identity Theft does not necessarily involve the use of computers or information and communication technology (ICT), electronic means have almost certainly developed into a primary method.

Since the creation of the NIBRS, a data element in the Offender segment—currently dubbed Data Element 8, Offender Suspected of Using—has seemed to permit coding offenses as being computer-related in their conduct through the option of "Computer Equipment." However, the variable has always been curiously defined, fusing an offender's suspected use of alcohol or drugs—two factors that potentially speak to an offender's alertness or impairment during the offense—with "Computer Equipment," a factor related to the general method of attack. As Appendix C notes, though, the extent to which Data Element 8 functions (or is meant to function) as a partial flag of cybercrime is an open question, as the most recent version of the NIBRS user manual describes the response option as Offender Suspected of Using "Computer Equipment (Handheld Devices)" and the only examples of the element's use related to fatalities involving distracted driving/driving while texting. Thus, the intent of Data Element 8 pertinent to potential cybercrime involvement is unclear.

In addition to approving the new Hacking/Computer Invasion and Identity Theft categories, the FBI director approved the addition of code 58, Cyberspace, as a potential response to Data Element 9's query for the location of the offense. A column in Table 2-1 indicates the NIBRS offenses that the most recent version of the NIBRS Technical Specification (Federal Bureau of Investigation, 2023a) indicates as eligible to use the Cyberspace code. However, since its introduction as a location response option, the user manual's examples on the application of the Cyberspace code (detailed in Appendix C) clearly denote the *internet* as integral to the offense, not just computer or information technology in general (excluding, for instance, computers in isolation or in local corporate intranets).

Table 2-3 presents a basic tabulation of these two principal computer-related indicators (i.e., Offender Suspected of Using Computer Equipment and Cyberspace as Location) from the 2022 public-use NIBRS Incident File, by the first offense coded in the record. The table is meant as a rough indicator of how often the two cues are used in isolation and in combination, and not as a definitive estimate of cybercrime prevalence as measured in 2022 NIBRS data. Our general impression is that there is some possible cybercrime signal in both cues but also considerable noise. For example, Cyberspace is listed as the location for many offenses for which the NIBRS Technical Specifications say the value is ineligible (e.g., rape and both aggravated and simple assault). For some offenses—Intimidation, Hacking/Computer Invasion, Wire Fraud, False Pretenses/Swindle/

TABLE 2-3 Current Use of Computer-Related Indicators in National Incident-Based Reporting System, 2022

NIBRS Code	NIBRS Offense Name	Cyberspace as Location	Data Element 8 Offender Suspected of Using Computer Equipment	Both Indicators
09A	Murder/Nonnegligent Manslaughter	0	35	0
09B	Negligent Manslaughter	0	3	0
09C	Justifiable Homicide	0	1	0
11A	Rape	32	319	11
11B	Sodomy	20	106	1
11C	Sexual Assault with an Object	7	34	1
11D	Fondling (Indecent Liberties/Child Molesting)	45	474	22
13A	Aggravated Assault	24	666	6
13B	Simple Assault	72	2,005	25
13C	Intimidation	16,652	16,020	3,923
23A	Pocket-picking	20	165	7
23B	Purse-snatching	8	23	3
23C	Shoplifting	9	611	2
23D	Theft from Building	372	1,086	134
23E	Theft from Coin-Operated Machine or Device	0	18	0
23F	Theft from Motor Vehicle	480	994	103
23G	Theft of Motor Vehicle Parts/Accessories	6	150	3
23H	All Other Larceny	1,599	10,048	502
26A	False Pretenses/Swindle/Confidence Game	29,742	22,210	7,946
26B	Credit Card/Automatic Teller Machine Fraud	13,507	8,291	3,122
26C	Impersonation	6,305	3,833	1,427
26D	Welfare Fraud	416	176	59
26E	Wire Fraud	11,530	8,597	4,952
26F	Identity Theft	23,305	13,436	6,232
26G	Hacking/Computer Invasion	1,714	1,921	823

continued

TABLE 2-3 Continued

NIBRS Code	NIBRS Offense Name	Cyberspace as Location	Data Element 8 Offender Suspected of Using Computer Equipment	Both Indicators
35A	Drug/Narcotic Violations	60	1,605	14
35B	Drug Equipment Violations	5	102	3
36A	Incest	3	18	3
36B	Statutory Rape	15	146	8
39A	Betting/Wagering	2	16	0
39B	Operating/Promoting/Assisting Gambling, Gambling Equipment	4	43	1
39C	Violations	0	28	0
39D	Sports Tampering	0	0	0
40A	Prostitution	59	73	15
40B	Assisting or Promoting Prostitution	39	131	18
40C	Purchasing Prostitution	16	105	5
64A	Human Trafficking—Commercial Sex Acts	62	126	24
64B	Human Trafficking—Involuntary Servitude	5	14	4
100	Kidnapping/Abduction	20	133	10
120	Robbery	21	277	4
200	Arson	0	19	0
210	Extortion/Blackmail	5,140	4,769	2,062
220	Burglary/Breaking and Entering	104	780	25
240	Motor Vehicle Theft	40	530	11
250	Counterfeiting/Forgery	2,646	3,917	726
270	Embezzlement	284	644	52
280	Stolen Property Offenses	49	212	7
290	Destruction/Damage/Vandalism of Property	37	772	9
370	Pornography/Obscene Material	6,922	9,567	2,556
510	Bribery	23	21	5
520	Weapon Law Violations	18	203	3
720	Animal Cruelty	0	11	0
	Overall Total	121,439	115,484	34,869

continued

TABLE 2-3 Continued

NOTES: National Incident-Based Reporting System (NIBRS) offenses listed in this table are the first offenses listed in the incident file. This simplification is used because the records in which either of the computer-use variables are applied tend to involve only one offense in the incident (92% of records with Cyberspace as Location, 89% of records in which offender is suspected of using computer equipment, and 89% with both). A total of 11,207,634 NIBRS incidents exist on the file. Federal agencies are not included in the data file, and hence the table omits entries for offenses eligible for reporting by federal and tribal law enforcement agencies only: 26H Money Laundering, 30A Illegal Entry into the United States, 30B False Citizenship, 30C Smuggling Illegal Aliens, 30D Re-entry after Deportation, 49A Fugitive (Harboring Escapee/Concealing from Arrest), 49B Flight to Avoid Prosecution, 49C Flight to Avoid Deportation, 58A Import Violations, 58B Export Violations, 61A Federal Liquor Offenses, 61B Federal Tobacco Offenses, 101 Treason, 103 Espionage, 360 Failure to Register as Sex Offender, 521 Violation of National Firearms Act of 1934, 522 Weapons of Mass Destruction, 526 Explosives Violations, and 620 Wildlife Trafficking.
SOURCE: Tabulation by panel member Lynn Addington from 2022 NIBRS Incident File (Bureau of Justice Statistics, 2023).

Confidence Game, Extortion/Blackmail, and Pornography/Obscene Material—the two variables could seemingly be interpreted as duplicative: very roughly equal shares applying each of the two data element indicators and a sizable number of those cases applying both. However, other crimes split differently. The interpersonal "street crimes" for which one of the computer indicators is selected (e.g., Rape, Assault, Theft from Building or Motor Vehicle, All Other Larceny, and Drug/Narcotic Violations) use the Data Element 8 Offender Suspected of Using Computer Equipment option more frequently, while the balance swings toward Cyberspace as Location for offenses like Credit Card/Automatic Teller Machine Fraud, Impersonation, and Identity Theft. We return to this point in Chapter 4, suggesting the need for reexamination and assessment of the definition and intended role of both the Cyberspace as Location and Offender Suspected of Using Computer Equipment cues.

CYBERCRIME HANDLING IN THE NATIONAL CRIME VICTIMIZATION SURVEY AND ITS SUPPLEMENTS

The core National Crime Victimization Survey (NCVS), operated by the Bureau of Justice Statistics (BJS) with the U.S. Census Bureau as data-collection agent, is a panel household survey that employs a multistage sampling design to collect data on criminal victimization incidents, regardless of whether they were reported to local law enforcement agencies. The first-stage sample of primary sampling units—counties, groups of counties, or metropolitan areas—is performed every 10 years, several years after the most recent decennial census. The second-stage sample of housing unit addresses (housing units) is drawn each year, with selected addresses remaining in-sample for three years (and, hence, for up to seven interviews on six-month intervals).[4] The NCVS uses computer-assisted personal interviews for initial interviews and a mix of computer-assisted personal interviews and computer-assisted telephone interviews for subsequent interviews.

NCVS interviews begin with the interviewer asking questions of a primary respondent (dubbed the household respondent) to build a roster of household members to determine their eligibility for interview, using the NCVS-500 Control Card instrument. The NCVS seeks interviews with each member of the household age 12 or older, only permitting proxy interviews in very limited circumstances. In these interviews with household members, the NCVS-1 Basic Screen Questionnaire asks respondents to recall potential victimizations over the six-month period prior to the interview; if the victimization is one of the offense types measured by the NCVS, then the interview continues with a detailed NCVS-2 Crime Incident Report questionnaire on each incident. The questions are asked with considerable care by trained interviewers, with the aim of eliciting an accurate and complete accounting of victimizations without unduly burdening or revictimizing the respondent. To the extent possible, interviews are also performed without requiring respondents to label the crime themselves (e.g., not directly asking if the respondent was the victim of an aggravated assault), instead eliciting enough information to allow construction of the proper offense type in subsequent data processing.

The great strength of the NCVS approach is that it gathers information about crime victimizations whether or not the incidents were reported to SLTT law enforcement agencies. Thus, the NCVS serves as a complement to police-report statistics like those of UCR/NIBRS. UCR and NCVS estimates are complementary, nonredundant measures, and comparison between the sources and their trends provides a more comprehensive view of crime in the United States. However, the resulting insight into the "dark figure of crime" not reported to police (Biderman & Reiss, 1967) depends upon the aptness of the comparison between the UCR and the NCVS, namely the consistency of definitions and concepts between the two sources. The NCVS began (as the National Crime Surveys) in the 1970s, and so its essential point of comparison was—and largely remains—the Part I offenses of the UCR SRS. Accordingly, the underlying crime classification used in

---

[4]The NCVS also includes a sample of group quarters (GQ) locations that is drawn from the first-stage primary sampling units every three years. Only certain types of noninstitutional GQs are eligible for inclusion, including college housing, group homes, and workers' quarters and dormitories; institutional GQs such as correctional facilities and skilled nursing facilities, as well as other noninstitutional GQs like military quarters, shelters, and maritime vessels, are out-of-scope for the NCVS (Bureau of Justice Statistics, 2017).

NCVS processing, shown in Box 2-2, is consistent with the "street-crime" focus of SRS crime categorization in Box 2-1, with the addition of Purse Snatching/Pocket Picking and—the NCVS being premised on self-reported victimization incidents—the exclusion of homicide. There are important practical reasons for keeping the core NCVS focused on a relatively small set of crimes, including time burden and facilitating cooperation with survey respondents. Asking additional questions on the NCVS-1 Basic Screen Questionnaire lengthens the time of the interviews, particularly if those questions elicit additional victimization instances that would be subject to the same detailed NCVS-2 Crime Incident Report questionnaire.

The NCVS has a long-standing penchant for improvement and reinvention; a major redesign in the early 1990s occasioned the formal name change from the National Crime Survey to the current NCVS, with a simultaneous retooling of the Basic-Screen-Questionnaire-and-Incident-Report approach. The 2024 NCVS will contain new instruments following another multiyear redesign, again aiming to increase the amount of contextual information captured in the interview while making the experience as easy as possible for respondents. So, in the context of cybercrime measurement, it is important to recognize that the NCVS did critical early work in this area. Figure 2-1 displays the bank of computer crime questionnaires that was included in the NCVS-1 Basic Screen Questionnaire between 2001 and 2004, emphasizing individuals' experiences with computer-related crimes in the context of personal use, not work-related use (unless in operation of a home business). The question set prompted respondents to recall five types of computer-related crime—fraud in an online purchase, computer virus, threats by online messaging or email, unrequested obscene communications via online means, and software copyright violation, as well as a write-in category for other computer-related crimes. However, the computer crime questions did not request a count of such incidents, overall or by type, and reports of these computer-related incidents did not trigger completion of an NCVS-2 Crime Incident Report. The questions were added in July 2001 and removed in July 2004 (Bureau of Justice Statistics, 2017, p. 53), and analyses of the resulting data do not appear to have factored into the BJS's Criminal Victimization report series during the period.

The primary means by which the NCVS program has expanded its substantive reach—and ventured into the measurement of cybercrime concepts—is the periodic fielding of supplemental modules of questions. These supplements may be administered to NCVS respondents if they meet eligibility criteria, even if they have no crime incidents to report in the core NCVS survey. As summarized in Table 2-4, three supplements have comprised the main source of cybercrime-related content for the NCVS following the 2004 discontinuation of the computer crime questions; a fourth supplement, the School Crime Supplement (SCS), touches on the particular

> **BOX 2-2**
> **Crime Classification in the National Crime Victimization Survey, 2017**
>
> **Personal Crimes**
> Crimes of Violence
>   Completed
>   Attempted
> Serious violent crimes
> Rape/sexual assault
>   Rape
>   Completed
>   Attempted
>   Sexual assault
> Robbery
>   Completed
>   With injury
>   Without injury
>   Attempted
>   With injury
>   Without injury
> Assault
>   Aggravated
>   Completed with injury
>   Attempted/threatened with weapon
>   Simple
>   Completed with injury
>   Attempted/threatened without weapon
> Purse snatching/pocket picking
>   Completed purse snatching
>   Attempted purse snatching
>   Pocket picking

incidence of bullying (which is typically not considered a crime in itself) and cyberbullying (which is more commonly defined as a crime).

We briefly describe these major cybercrime-related supplements in the following subsections, and one cross-cutting theme is worth noting first. The 2001–2004 NCVS-1 Basic Screen Questionnaire items on computer crime (Figure 2-1) include one that hints at a unique strength of the survey approach to measuring crime and cybercrime: in addition to providing insight on incidents that were not reported to law enforcement or other authorities, it can also suggest reasons why the incidents were not reported. This feature has also been utilized in subsequent cybercrime-related supplements. Box 2-3 presents a composite listing of response options for the

Property Crimes
Burglary
  Completed
    Forcible entry
    Unlawful entry without force
  Attempted forcible entry
Motor vehicle theft
  Completed
  Attempted
Theft
  Completed
    Less than $50
    $50–$249
    $250 or more
    Amount not available
  Attempted

NOTES: Serious violent crimes include Rape/sexual assault, Robbery, and Aggravated assault. Relative to the original source, level of indent has been changed for Crimes of violence/Completed and Attempted and for Theft/Completed/Amount not available as the original source apparently contained formatting errors. No subdivision of Serious violent crimes (i.e., Completed or Attempted) appears in the source, so none is added here.
SOURCE: Bureau of Justice Statistics (2017, Table 1).

question on why an offense was not reported to local law enforcement or other authorities from the two most recent iterations of the Identity Theft Supplement (ITS) and Supplemental Fraud Survey (SFS), to illustrate the valuable contextual information that can be derived from survey work.

Identity Theft, Fraud, and the Identity Theft Supplement and Supplemental Fraud Survey

The Federal Trade Commission (FTC) began collecting consumer complaints in its Consumer Sentinel Network in 1997, and shortly thereafter received statutory authority to serve as the centralized complaint and

HOUSEHOLD RESPONDENT'S COMPUTER CRIME SCREEN QUESTIONS	
FIELD REPRESENTATIVE – Read introduction. INTRO: The next series of questions are about YOUR use of a computer. Please include ALL computers, laptops, or access to WebTV used at home, work, or school for PERSONAL USE or for operating a home business.	

45c. During the last 6 months, have YOU used a computer, laptop, or WebTV for the following purposes (Read answer categories 1–4) –
Mark (X) all that apply.
	100 1 ☐ For personal use at home?
	        2 ☐ For personal use at work?
	        3 ☐ For personal use at school, libraries, etc.?
	        4 ☐ To operate a home business?
	        5 ☐ None of the above – SKIP to Check Item D

45d. How many computers do you have access to for personal use or for operating a home business?	101 0 ☐ None
	        1 ☐ 1
	        2 ☐ 2
	        3 ☐ 3
	        4 ☐ 4 or more

45e. Do YOU use the Internet for personal use or for operating a home business?	102 1 ☐ Personal use
	        2 ☐ Operating a home business
	        3 ☐ Both
	        4 ☐ None of the above

45f. Have you experienced any of the following COMPUTER-RELATED incidents in the last 6 months (Read answer categories 1–6) –
Mark (X) all that apply.
	103 1 ☐ Fraud in purchasing something over the Internet?
	        2 ☐ Computer virus attack?
	        3 ☐ Threats of harm or physical attack made while online or through E-mail?
	        4 ☐ Unrequested lewd or obscene messages, communications, or images while online or through E-mail?
	        5 ☐ (Only ask if box 4 is marked in Item 45c) Software copyright violation in connection with a home business?
	        6 ☐ Something else that you consider a computer-related crime?–Specify ⤵
	        _____
	        7 ☐ No computer-related incidents –SKIP to Check Item D

45g. Did you suffer any monetary loss as a result of the incident(s) you just mentioned?	104 1 ☐ Yes 2 ☐ No – SKIP to 45i
45h. How much money did you lose as a result of the incident(s)?	105 $ _____ .00 Amount of loss x ☐ Don't know

45i. Did you report the incident(s) you just mentioned to (Read answer categories 1 –5) –
Mark (X) all that apply.
	106 1 ☐ A law enforcement agency?
	        2 ☐ An Internet Service provider?
	        3 ☐ A Website administrator?
	        4 ☐ A Systems Administrator?
	        5 ☐ Someone else? – Specify ⤵
	        _____
	        6 ☐ None of the above

FIGURE 2-1 Computer crime questions on the National Crime Victimization Survey, 2001–2004.
NOTES: Excerpt shows the questions administered to the primary respondent, known as the household respondent. The same questions were asked of each individual respondent in the household. No count of computer crime incidents was elicited in this set of questions; consequently, the follow-up NCVS-2 Crime Incident Report was not completed for any computer crime incident.
SOURCE: Excerpt from page 16 of Form NCVS-1 (5-10-2001), the National Crime Victimization Survey NCVS-1 Basic Screen Questionnaire (OMB No. 1121-0111, approval expiring 10/31/2003); https://bjs.ojp.gov/content/pub/pdf/ncvs1.pdf

TABLE 2-4 Overview of Cybercrime-Related Supplements to the National Crime Victimization Survey

Supplement Name	Dates Conducted	Universe of Interest	Topic
Identity Theft Supplement (ITS)	2021, 2018, 2016, 2014, 2012, 2008	NCVS respondents age 16 and older; some questions reference all such identity theft experienced in past 12 months, but detailed questions limited to single most recent incident; closing question asks whether respondent has ever been notified that their information has been part of a data breach	Identity theft/misuse of personal information of three basic varieties: misuse of an existing account (i.e., credit card/bank/email or social media/other), opening a new account, or other fraudulent purposes; respondents are asked how they think the personal information was obtained, which includes cyber/computer-related options
Supplemental Fraud Survey (SFS)	2017	NCVS respondents age 18 and older; fraud must have been completed (money must have been lost) to count; some questions reference all such fraud experienced in past 12 months, but detailed questions limited to single most recent incident	Seven types of personal financial fraud (i.e., prize or grant fraud, phantom debt collection fraud, charity fraud, employment fraud, consumer investment fraud, consumer products or services fraud, and relationship/trust fraud); cyber/computer involvement in conduct of the fraud not asked explicitly but implied more strongly for some types (e.g., most categories describing how the relationship/trust fraud was conducted are online/social media or electronic communication in nature; question as to whether charity fraud payments were made through a crowdfunding website)
Supplemental Victimization Survey (SVS)	2019, 2016, 2006	NCVS respondents age 18 and older (2006) and age 16 and older (2016 and subsequent)	Stalking, harassment, and other unwanted contact/behavior; questions ask about contacts/behaviors via social media, internet, phone, or other technology, and thus encompass cyberstalking and cyberharassment

NOTE: NCVS, National Crime Victimization Survey.
SOURCE: Adapted and updated from Bureau of Justice Statistics (2017) through reference to individual supplement pages and questionnaires at https://bjs.ojp.gov/data-collections/search

> **BOX 2-3**
> **Response Options for Why Incident
> Was Not Reported to Law Enforcement,
> 2017 Supplemental Fraud Survey and
> 2021 Identity Theft Supplement**
>
> **Didn't Know (SFS[a])/Didn't Know I Could (ITS[b])**
> - Didn't know I could (or should) report it/wasn't sure it was a crime (SFS[a])/Didn't know that I could report it (ITS[b])
> - Didn't know how to contact them (SFS[a])
> - Didn't know who to contact (SFS[a])
> - Didn't think about reporting it (ITS[b])
> - Didn't know what agency was responsible for identity theft crimes (ITS[b])
>
> **Not Important Enough**
> - Didn't lose much money or got most of money back (SFS[a])
> - I didn't lose any money (ITS[b])
> - Not important enough to report/small loss (ITS[b])
>
> **Handled It Another Way (ITS[b])/Took Care of It Myself (SFS[a])**
> - Took care of it myself
> - Credit card company/other organization took care of the problem (ITS[b])
>
> **Didn't Think Police Could Help**
> - Didn't think it would do any good (SFS[a])/Didn't think police would do anything (ITS[b])
> - Didn't want to bother police (ITS[b])

consumer resource clearinghouse for victims of identity theft. Broadening its study of the problem, the FTC commissioned Synovate (2003) to conduct a telephone household survey in March–April 2003, asking about incidences of identity theft, victims' experiences, and whether incidents were reported to any authorities. A National Institute of Justice–funded review of data-collection work by Newman and McNally (2005) commended the pioneering FTC work and noted the lack of a centralized criminal justice database on identity theft and fraud incidents. This review spurred additional data-collection efforts associated with the NCVS.

In 2004, the respondent-level computer crime questions were removed from the NCVS-1 Basic Screen Questionnaire and a new set of 10 identity theft questions was added. As with the computer crime questions, reported identity theft instances were not subject to the detailed NCVS-2 Crime Incident Report questionnaire; however, the identity theft questions were household level, and thus only the principal household respondent was

- Found out about the incident too late (SFS[a])
- Didn't find out about the crime until long after it happened/too late for police to help (ITS[b])
- Occurred in another state or outside of the United States (ITS[b])
- Couldn't provide much information about the offender (SFS[a])/Couldn't identify the offender or provide much information that would be helpful to the police (ITS[b])

Personal Reasons
- Didn't want to have any contact with the police (SFS[a])
- Didn't want to get offender in trouble (SFS[a])/The person responsible was a friend or family member, and I didn't want to get them in trouble (ITS[b])
- I was too embarrassed/ashamed (SFS[a])
- Too inconvenient/didn't want to take the time

[a]SFS, Supplemental Fraud Survey.
[b]ITS, Identity Theft Supplement.
NOTE: Responses/phrases without a tag are found in both supplements. The SFS also asks why the incident was not reported to a financial institution, the Better Business Bureau, or some other entity; the response options are the same as for this question about reporting to law enforcement except that the "Didn't want to have any contact with the police" option is omitted.
SOURCE: Panel generated from survey questionnaires at https://bjs.ojp.gov/document/itsq21.pdf and https://bjs.ojp.gov/content/pub/pdf/sfs_2017.pdf

asked to describe any such "episodes of identity theft discovered by you or anyone in your household during the last 6 months."[5] The questions focused on three principal variants of identity theft: (a) misuse of an existing credit card account, (b) misuse of some other type of existing account, or (c) attempt to use personal information to open a new account (credit card or other). Follow-up questions asked whether the incident occurred once or in combination with other identity theft attempts, the amount lost, whether the misuse caused subsequent hardship (e.g., being turned down for loans), and how the victim became aware of the theft. Curiously, though, the questionnaire did not ask whether the incident was reported. The questions remained on the NCVS-1 Basic Screen Questionnaire into 2008, and the BJS issued two reports from these early efforts at national-level estimates (Baum, 2006, 2007).

---
[5]See https://bjs.ojp.gov/content/pub/pdf/ncvs104.pdf

In 2008, the set of identity theft questions was converted into a new rotating supplement to be added to the NCVS for six-month periods (Langton & Planty, 2010). The initial 2008 ITS expanded to include 67 questions in several module groups, including modules on how and when the identity theft was discovered, how the victim responded (e.g., report to authorities and to credit bureaus and satisfaction with the response), emotional impact on the victim, known information on the offender (e.g., relationship to victim), financial impact, knowledge of attempted-but-failed instances of identity theft over the past two years, and risk avoidance (i.e., measures taken in reaction to the identity theft).[6] The ITS has now been fielded six times, retaining the same basic structure. Specifically regarding cybercrime, the ITS's reference to cyber or computer involvement in the offense is not overt. However, from the first ITS to the most recent iteration in 2021,[7] the ITS questionnaire has typically ended with some cyber-related questions as context. A question on whether the respondent purchased anything via the internet in the past year has dropped off, perhaps reflecting the ubiquity of ecommerce, but ITS iterations have all generally asked respondents if they have ever been notified of their personal information being involved in a data breach.

Similar to identity theft, the BJS's extension of the NCVS to probe consumer fraud came after valuable initial telephone survey work sponsored by the FTC, conducted in 2003, 2005, 2011, and 2017.[8] For its own SFS to the NCVS, fielded in October–December 2017, the BJS set out to study seven specific types of financial fraud, representing the top-level categories of financial fraud against individuals in a taxonomy for financial fraud developed by the Stanford Financial Fraud Research Center and the FINRA Foundation (Beals et al., 2015).[9] These seven types, based on the purported benefit underlying the fraud, are prize or grant, phantom debt collection, charity, employment, consumer investment, consumer products or services, and relationship/trust fraud. To count an incident as fraud, the 2017 SFS required that the fraud must have been completed and the victim must have lost money (Bureau of Justice Statistics, 2017, p. 12). The SFS questionnaire is designed like an NCVS in a microcosm, with a screen questionnaire eliciting recall of incidents of each of the seven types of fraud (while also endeavoring to avoid using the word "fraud") followed by an incident report to gather more detailed information. Specifically in terms of cybercrime, it is

---

[6] See https://bjs.ojp.gov/content/pub/pdf/its_08.pdf

[7] See https://bjs.ojp.gov/document/itsq21.pdf

[8] See https://www.ftc.gov/news-events/news/press-releases/2019/10/ftc-releases-results-2017-mass-market-consumer-fraud-survey

[9] The Beals et al. (2015) taxonomy was also a basis for the specification of fraud as an offense in the National Academies of Sciences, Engineering, and Medicine (2016a, pp. 144–148) classification of crime for statistical purposes.

important to note that the method by which the fraud was perpetrated is not directly asked in the SFS questionnaire but arises indirectly for some specific fraud types: the Charity Fraud incident report asks whether a crowdfunding website was used, and most of the response options describing how first contact was made in a Relationship/Trust Fraud incident are electronic or social media–related.[10]

The BJS summarized the resulting data from the 2017 SFS in its own report (Morgan, 2021) and commissioned a separate review of the quality of the supplement by Langton et al. (2023), which included comparison with estimates of fraud from numerous other sources, including the NIBRS and the predecessor surveys. The 2017 SFS remains the only administration of the supplement as of late 2024, likely owing to the principal, unusual result studied by the Langton et al. (2023) review: estimates of individual financial fraud in other data sources range widely (and may include differences in defining covered fraud types), but the SFS's estimate of 1.2 percent of persons age 18 or older experiencing financial fraud in 2017 seems small relative to other reported estimates. That said, another round of the SFS is reported to be forthcoming at the time of this writing.

Cyberstalking and the Supplemental Victimization Survey

The Office on Violence Against Women sponsored the first Supplemental Victimization Survey (SVS) to the NCVS in 2006 to measure stalking, and the supplement has since been administered in 2016 and 2019. The best way to portray the crime content and basic approach of the SVS is to review the first (screener) question on the instrument that the NCVS/SVS interviewer reads to any NCVS respondent age 16 or older (see Box 2-4).[11] The first notable feature of the question is that it spells out a detailed 12-part classification of types of stalking behaviors—incidences and consequences of which are discussed in the rest of the survey—without actually using the word "stalking" to avoid any unwanted connotations or instinctual reactions. Second, the embedded classification of stalking behaviors has two higher-level categories. Responses a–f are "traditional," mainly physical stalking behaviors, including direct physical surveillance, while responses g–l all fall under the general heading of "stalking with technology." The report on the outcomes of the 2019 SVS emphasizes that cyberstalking (as defined in federal law; see Appendix C) and stalking with technology are very close in concept but not identical—the essential difference being that the text messages clause in Box 2-4 item g would likely be covered

---

[10] See https://bjs.ojp.gov/content/pub/pdf/sfs_2017.pdf
[11] The minimum response age was lowered from 18 to 16 for the second and subsequent administrations of the SVS.

> **BOX 2-4**
> **Question 1, Types of Stalking Behaviors Measured, Supplemental Victimization Survey, 2019**
>
> Now, I would like to ask you some questions about the times when you may have experienced unwanted contacts or behaviors. I want to remind you that the information you provide is confidential. When answering, please think about anyone who may have done these things, including current or former spouses or partners, other people you may know, or strangers. However, please DO NOT include bill collectors, solicitors, or other sales people.
>
> **SQ1**. In the past 12 months, have you experienced any unwanted contacts or behaviors? By that I mean . . .
>   a. Has anyone followed you around and watched you?
>   b. Has anyone snuck into your home, car, or any place else and done unwanted things to let you know they had been there?
>   c. Has anyone waited for you at home, work, school, or any place else when you didn't want them to?
>
> Still thinking about unwanted contacts and behaviors, in the past 12 months . . .
>   d. Has anyone shown up, ridden or driven by places where you were when they had no business being there?
>   e. Has anyone left or sent unwanted items, such as cards, letters, presents, flowers, or any other unwanted items?
>   f. Has anyone harassed or repeatedly asked your friends or family for information about you or your whereabouts?

by definitions of cyberstalking, but the pure telephone and voice message contact modes in item g might not (Morgan & Truman, 2019, p. 3).

Federal law describes two other essential elements to the definition of stalking/cyberstalking (18 U.S.C. § 2261A(2); see Appendix C), and incorporating these elements affects the way the SVS proceeds. First, like the general offense of harassment, stalking/cyberstalking is a repeated-course-of-conduct offense, meaning that a single instance of the stalking behaviors in Box 2-4 does not constitute a stalking/cyberstalking offense; there must be two or more instances.[12] Second, the course-of-conduct actions must produce either actual fear (i.e., substantial emotional distress) or reasonable fear (i.e., threatened or completed attack on the victim, someone close to the victim, or a pet, sufficient to cause fear for their safety). In administrations to date, the SVS has taken a slightly unusual approach to the course-of-conduct problem,

---

[12]This is the case even with the plural forms of key nouns in the Box 2-4 options, such as the "phone calls" and "text messages" of option g and "e-mails or messages" of option k.

> Now I want to ask about unwanted contacts and behaviors using various technologies, such as your phone, the Internet, or social media apps. Again, please DO NOT include bill collectors, solicitors, or other unwanted sales people. In the past 12 months . . .
> g. Has anyone made unwanted phone calls to you, left voice messages, sent text messages, or used the phone excessively to contact you?
> h. Has anyone spied on you or monitored your activities using technologies such as a listening device, camera, or computer or cell phone monitoring software?
>
> Still thinking about unwanted contacts and behaviors, in the past 12 months . . .
> i. Has anyone tracked your whereabout with an electronic tracking device or application, such as GPS or an application on your cell phone?
> j. Has anyone posted or threatened to post inappropriate, unwanted, or personal information about you on the Internet, including private photographs, videos, or spreading rumors?
> k. Has anyone sent you unwanted e-mails or messages using the Internet, for example, using social media apps or websites like Instagram, Twitter, or Facebook?
> l. Has anyone monitored your activities using social media apps like Instagram, Twitter, or Facebook?
>
> SOURCE: Excerpted (less variable names and Yes/No response boxes to each question) from 2019 Supplemental Victimization Survey questionnaire, https://bjs.ojp.gov/content/pub/pdf/svs_19.pdf

defined as the repeated occurrence of one of the specific stalking behaviors depicted in Box 2-4 (as determined by a follow-up question if only one "Yes" response is received) or the occurrence of multiple stalking behaviors (Morgan & Truman, 2019, p. 3). The SVS asks a follow-up question as to whether any of the experienced stalking behaviors caused actual fear and, similarly, whether any caused reasonable fear. If the course of conduct and either actual or reasonable fear are established, the respondent is queried about the details of the incident, including knowledge of the offender(s), purported motive, and whether the incident was reported to authorities.

Cyberbullying and the School Crime Supplement

The recurring SCS to the NCVS is the product of a long-standing partnership between the BJS and the National Center for Education Statistics in the U.S. Department of Education. The SCS, which has been administered on a roughly biennial cycle since 1999 (and fielded twice previously in 1989 and 1995), has always included some content related to bullying. The SCS bullying content was revised in the 2005 administration of the supplement, to ask about bullying behaviors in a manner more consistent with definitions under joint development by the U.S. Department of Education and the U.S. Centers for Disease Control and Prevention (CDC; Gladden et al., 2014).[13] Though some bullying behaviors mentioned in earlier versions of the SCS could arguably be carried out by electronic/computer means, it was not until the 2022 SCS that changes were made aiming to better capture cyberbullying (or electronic bullying, as it is labeled by Gladden et al. [2014]). These changes included revising the introduction to the main bullying question to say that "these [unwanted behaviors] could occur in person or using technologies, such as a phone, the Internet, or social media"[14] and the addition of a separate category for "purposely shared your private information, photos, or videos in a hurtful way."[15] Note, however, that the changes served to capture more electronic bullying behavior but did not necessarily distinguish it from conventional bullying; the distinction remains murky in that some of the other bullying behaviors (e.g., "made fun of you, called you names, or insulted you in a hurtful way" or "spread rumors about you") could occur by either electronic or nonelectronic means. The results of the most recent administration of the SCS, in 2022, are summarized by Irvin et al. (2024).

Two general points about bullying and cyberbullying are worthy of brief mention in the context of current data sources. First, bullying is necessarily a difficult concept for national crime statistics because there is wide variation in the degree to which the states classify and consider bullying a crime in their penal or criminal codes, as opposed to regulating the behavior under the state's education code. Likewise, there is variation in the ways in which cyberbullying—if called out specifically in state law—is handled, though some states directly criminalize cyberbullying because of the potential for adults to perform the bullying actions while posing as

---

[13] Prior to deployment, the questions were cognitively tested by U.S. Census Bureau staff (Pascale et al., 2014).

[14] Previously, as in the 2019 version of the SCS, a question about where the bullying incidents occurred listed "Online or by text" as a response option; see https://bjs.ojp.gov/sites/g/files/xyckuh236/files/media/survey/2019_scs.pdf. The location question was not asked in the 2022 questionnaire, part of broadening the supplement's scope from the traditional "at school" to the more inclusive "during school."

[15] See https://bjs.ojp.gov/sites/g/files/xyckuh236/files/media/survey/2022_scs.pdf. Another category/response in the main bullying question, number 22 on the questionnaire, makes explicit mention of social media: "excluded you from activities, social media, or other communications to hurt you."

juveniles on social media and electronic forums.[16] Second, as types of behavior that straddle the line between criminal and education/civil law, bullying and cyberbullying are covered to some extent in other educational and public health data surveillance systems, including the Youth Risk Behavior Survey coordinated by the CDC, the Health Behaviour in School-Aged Children Survey coordinated by the World Health Organization, and the National Survey of Children's Exposure to Violence jointly sponsored by the U.S. Department of Justice and the CDC (National Academies, 2016b).

Cybercrime Against Businesses, and the National Computer Security Survey

For purposes of measuring cybercrime, the major drawback of the NCVS and its supplements is that, being household surveys, they only examine offenses against survey respondents—individual persons, not businesses or organizations. This was not always the case, however. As described in more detail by the National Research Council (2008), the NCVS began in 1972 as the National Crime Surveys—plural—and included two commercial components, a national sample of 15,000 businesses and targeted samples of 2,000 businesses in 26 cities (data were only collected from eight of the focus cities at a time). However, an early review by an even more distant predecessor of our panel (National Research Council, 1976) recommended that city-specific sampling be stopped in favor of boosting the national sample size of the household crime survey and also advised that the commercial victimization survey be suspended and reassessed. Combined with budgetary reasons and perceived inadequacy of the business sampling frame then in use, the commercial victimization component of the National Crime Surveys was eliminated shortly thereafter.

Interest in commercial victimization has resurfaced over the years, and the emergence of cybercrime spurred particular attention. In 2001, a second effort to measure crimes against businesses was cosponsored by the BJS and the National Cyber Security Division of the U.S. Department of Homeland Security (USDHS); RAND was engaged as the data-collection agent, and the

---

[16]For example, Louisiana Revised Statute 14:40.7 (added in 2010, revised 2019; Title 14 is Criminal Law) defines cyberbullying—"transmission of any electronic textual, visual, written, or oral communication with the malicious and willful intent to coerce, abuse, torment, or intimidate a person under the age of eighteen"—as a crime, punishable by fine or imprisonment when the offender is an adult but "governed exclusively by Title VII of the Children's Code" (i.e., the juvenile justice system) when the offender is under age 18. This overlaps with more wide-ranging anti-bullying laws enacted in 2022 and 2024 (Louisiana RS 17:416.14, Title 17 being the Education title of the statutes), including more detailed definitions and "electronic communication" as a means of bullying, but focused on establishing comprehensive policy within school districts rather than criminal sanctions for the offense.

survey was conducted first as a pilot and then in full in 2005. This effort, dubbed the National Computer Security Survey (NCSS), was developed to measure the nature and extent of computer security incidents, monetary costs, and other consequences. The specific types of incidents covered by the NCSS are shown in Box 2-5, and Box 2-6 shows that the NCSS also asked responding companies and organizations why incidents were or were not reported to law enforcement or other authorities. The survey collected data from 7,818 businesses. Although 67 percent of responding businesses detected cybercrime in 2005, most businesses did not report cyberattacks to law enforcement (Rantala, 2008).

Though the NCSS remains listed on the BJS's website as an active program, it has not been fielded since the single instance in 2005, possibly owing to a lower-than-expected response rate (23%) in the initial administration (Rantala, 2008, p. 15).

BOX 2-5
Types of Computer Security Incidents Covered by 2005 National Computer Security Survey

Cyber attack
- Computer virus—defined as "a hidden fragment of computer code which propagates by inserting itself into or modifying other programs." Meant to include worms, trojan horses, etc., but not spyware, adware, or other malware (which are to be included as "other computer security incidents").
- Denial of service—defined as "the disruption, degradation, or exhaustion of an Internet connection or e-mail service that results in an interruption of the normal flow of information. Denial of service is usually caused by ping attacks, port scanning probes, excessive amounts of incoming data, etc."
- Electronic vandalism or sabotage—defined as "the deliberate or malicious damage, defacement, destruction or other alteration of electronic files, data, web pages, programs, etc."

Cyber theft
- Embezzlement—defined as "the unlawful misappropriation of money or other things of value, BY THE PERSON TO WHOM IT WAS ENTRUSTED (typically an employee), for his/her own use or purpose. INCLUDE instances in which a computer was used to wrongfully transfer, counterfeit, forge or gain access to money, property, financial documents, insurance policies, deeds, use of rental cars, various services, etc., by the person to whom it was entrusted."

OTHER ENTITIES COLLECTING CYBERCRIME-RELATED DATA, PARTICULARLY FRAUD

Internet Crime Complaint Center

The FBI's Internet Crime Complaint Center (IC3) was originally founded as the Internet Fraud Complaint Center in 2000, adopting the current name and a broader focus in 2003. The IC3 primarily functions as an avenue for receiving complaints of internet-facilitated and internet-related crimes from the public. IC3 analysts assess the public reports for validity (U.S. Government Accountability Office, 2023). Commonly, the relevant financial institution is contacted (i.e., to ensure that no further harm has been done to the victim's account); the incident is also referred to the appropriate FBI field office, if necessary, for further

- Fraud—defined as "the intentional misrepresentation of information or identity to deceive others, the unlawful use of credit/debit card or ATM or the use of electronic means to transmit deceptive information, in order to obtain money or other things of value. Fraud may be committed by someone inside or outside the company. INCLUDE instances in which a computer was used by someone inside or outside this company in order to defraud this company of money, property, financial documents, insurance policies, deeds, use of rental cars, various services, etc., by means of forgery, misrepresented identity, credit card or wire fraud, etc."
- Theft of intellectual property—defined as "the illegal obtaining of copyrighted or patented material, trade secrets, or trademarks including designs, plans, blueprints, codes, computer programs, software, formulas, recipes, graphics, etc., usually by electronic copying."
- Theft of personal or financial data—defined as "the illegal obtaining of information that could potentially allow someone to use or create accounts under another name (individual, business, or some other entity). Personal information includes names, dates of birth, social security numbers, etc. Financial information includes credit/debit/ATM card, account, or PIN numbers, etc."

Other computer security incidents—to include "all other computer security incidents involving this company's computer networks—such as hacking, sniffing, spyware, theft of other information—regardless of whether damage or losses were sustained as a result."

SOURCES: Panel generated from survey questionnaire at https://bjs.ojp.gov/content/pub/pdf/ncss_1.pdf and Davis et al. (2008).

> **BOX 2-6**
> **Response Options on Reporting and Nonreporting of Computer Security Incidents, 2005 National Computer Security Survey**
>
> **To which of the following organizations were these incidents reported?** *Mark all that apply.*
> - Local law enforcement
> - State law enforcement
> - FBI (Federal Bureau of Investigation)
> - US-CERT (United States Computer Emergency Readiness Team)
> - CERT® Coordination Center
> - Other federal agency *(Specify)*
> - ISAC (Information Sharing and Analysis Center)
> - InfraGard
> - None of the above
>
> **If any incidents were not reported to the organizations specified [above], what were the reasons?** *Mark all that apply.*
> - Handled internally
> - Reported to third-party contractor providing computer security services
> - Reported to another organization *(Specify)*
> - Negative publicity
> - Lower customer/client/investor confidence
> - Competitor advantage
> - Did not want data/hardware seized as evidence
> - Did not know who to contact
> - Incident outside jurisdiction of law enforcement
> - Did not think to report
> - Nothing to be gained/nothing worth pursuing
> - Other *(Specify)*
>
> NOTE: Question text excerpted from section of questions related to occurrences of fraud, but similar/identical wording applies to other incident types.
> SOURCES: Panel generated from survey questionnaire at https://bjs.ojp.gov/content/pub/pdf/ncss_1.pdf and Davis et al. (2008).

investigation (Quigley, 2024). Complaints are submitted through the IC3 Network, which includes an online complaint referral form and an associated database of complaint information. The complaint form itself does not require the respondent to categorize the incident as a crime/cybercrime directly, but it provides an open-text field for response that analysts can fill in, based on the data provided, to classify the incident by type. An annual report (e.g., Federal Bureau of Investigation, 2023c,

2024) summarizes the number and geographical distribution of reported offenses, along with an estimate of the monetary losses incurred through the offenses. In 2023, IC3 received 880,418 complaints amounting to losses totaling $12.5 billion (Federal Bureau of Investigation, 2024).

The annual reports regularly contain a table showing reported offenses within the past three years; four years of these three-year tables are combined in Table 2-5 to convey the range of offenses covered by the IC3 and shifts in their categorization over time. Numerous variants of fraud (labeled by the purported benefit in the fraud) dominate the listings in IC3's reports, befitting the organization's original name, but other cybercrime types (e.g., ransomware, crimes against children, and harassment/stalking) are reported to IC3 by the public and hence show up in IC3 annual reports. There is no apparent underlying structure to the IC3's list of covered offenses, save that it shifts slightly from year to year and is revised based on changes in frequency of particular groups of offenses.

Federal Trade Commission's Consumer Sentinel Network

The FTC's Consumer Sentinel Network is a centralized database and repository for customer complaint data. While the IC3, initially established to monitor internet fraud, has expanded its scope to include other types of cybercrime, the FTC's collection remains focused, in extensive detail, on crimes of fraud and identity theft as well as related scams and bad business practices. The same law that defined the federal offense of identity theft (P.L. 105-318; see Appendix C) defined the FTC as the "centralized complaint and consumer education service for victims of identity theft," directing the FTC to "log and acknowledge" consumer complaints and to refer them to credit reporting agencies and law enforcement agencies as appropriate. The Consumer Sentinel Network database is populated by reports from the public through its online portal, but also extensively through data provided by other contributors (e.g., the IC3, the Better Business Bureau, the Consumer Financial Protection Bureau, and state attorneys general). In 2023, the FTC collected 2.6 million reports classified as fraud, with $10.3 billion in reported losses (Fletcher, 2024). Box 2-7 shows the top-level report categories defined in the Consumer Sentinel Network, including 17 categories for fraud and seven categories for identity theft, all based on the good or service the offender is attempting to collect through the fraud or identity theft. The companion list of Consumer Sentinel Network report subcategories[17] defines a pool of 97 goods, services, or other objectives of fraudulent activity. There is inherent fluidity to these categorizations; in discussion with the

---

[17] See https://www.ftc.gov/system/files/ftc_gov/pdf/CSNPSCFullDescriptions.pdf

TABLE 2-5 Victim Count in Crime Types Reported in Internet Crime Complaint Center Annual Reports, 2018–2023

Offense	Victim Count					
	2023	2022	2021	2020	2019	2018
Advanced Fee	8,045	11,264	11,034	13,020	14,607	16,362
BEC[a]	21,489	21,832	19,954	19,369	23,775	20,373
Botnet	540	568	—	—	—	—
Charity	—	—	—	659	407	493
Civil Matter	—	—	1,118	968	908	768
Confidence Fraud/Romance	17,823	19,021	24,299	23,751	19,473	18,493
Corporate Data Breach	—	—	1,287	2,794	1,795	2,480
Credit Card/Check Fraud[b]	13,718	22,985	16,750	17,614	14,378	15,210
Crimes Against Children	2,361	2,587	2,167	3,202	1,312	1,394
Data Breach	3,727	2,795	1,287	2,794	—	—
Denial of Service/TDoS	—	—	1,104	2,018	1,353	1,799
Employment	15,443	14,946	15,253	16,879	14,493	14,979
Extortion	48,223	39,416	39,360	76,741	43,101	51,146
Gambling	—	—	395	391	262	181
Government Impersonation	14,190	11,554	11,335	12,827	13,973	10,978
Hacktivist	—	—	—	52	39	77
Health Care Related	—	—	578	1,383	657	337
Identity Theft	19,778	27,922	51,629	43,330	16,053	16,128
Investment	39,570	30,529	20,561	8,788	3,999	3,693
IPR/Copyright and Counterfeit	1,498	2,183	4,270	4,213	3,892	2,249
Lottery/Sweepstakes/Inheritance	4,168	5,650	5,991	8,501	7,767	7,146
Malware[c]	659	762	810	1,423	2,373	2,811
Misrepresentation	—	—	—	24,276	5,975	5,959

Non-Payment/Non-Delivery	50,523	51,679	82,478	108,869	61,832	65,116
Other	8,808	9,966	12,346	10,372	10,842	10,826
Overpayment	4,144	6,183	6,108	10,988	15,395	15,512
Personal Data Breach	55,851	58,859	51,829	45,330	38,218	50,642
Phishing/Spoofing	*298,878*	*321,136*	*342,494*	*269,560*	*140,491*	*41,948*
Phishing[d]	—	300,497	323,972	241,342	114,702	26,379
Spoofing	—	20,649	18,522	28,218	25,789	15,569
Ransomware	2,825	2,385	3,729	2,474	2,047	1,493
Real Estate[e]	9,521	11,727	11,578	13,638	11,677	11,300
Re-Shipping	—	—	516	883	929	907
SIM Swap	1,075	2,026	—	—	—	—
Tech Support	37,560	32,538	23,903	15,421	13,633	14,408
Harassment/Stalking	9,587	11,779	—	—	—	—
Threats of Violence	1,697	2,224	—	—	—	—
Terrorism/Threats of Violence	—	—	12,346	20,669	15,563	—
Harassment/Threats of Violence	—	—	—	20,604	15,502	18,415
Terrorism	—	—	—	65	61	120

[a] Renamed BEC (Business Email Compromise) from BEC/EAC (latter meaning Email Account Compromise) in 2022 report.
[b] Check Fraud added to Credit Card Fraud in 2022 report.
[c] Renamed Malware from Malware/Scareware/Virus in 2022 report.
[d] Renamed Phishing from Phishing/Vishing/Smishing/Pharming in 2022 report.
[e] Renamed Real Estate from Real Estate/Rental in 2020 report.

NOTES: —, category not used in reporting year; IPR, intellectual property rights; TDoS, Telephony Denial of Service. Rows indicating the separate handling of harassment, terrorism, and threats of violence are grouped at the end, out of alphabetical order, for ease of comparison. The only added calculations are the italicized entries for Phishing/Spoofing in 2018, summing the individual Phishing and Spoofing entries because the two offense types were not previously reported as a combined sum.

SOURCES: Panel generated from "Last-Three-Year Complaint Comparison" table in *Internet Crime Report* issues for 2020–2023 (Federal Bureau of Investigation, 2021, 2022, 2023c, 2024).

> **BOX 2-7**
> **Report Categories in the Federal Trade Commission Consumer Sentinel Network**
>
> **Fraud**
> - Advance Payments for Credit Services
> - Business and Job Opportunities
> - Charitable Solicitations
> - Foreign Money Offers and Fake Check Scams
> - Grants
> - Health Care
> - Imposter Scams
> - Internet Services
> - Investment Related
> - Magazines and Books
> - Mortgage Foreclosure Relief and Debt Management
> - Office Supplies and Services
> - Online Shopping and Negative Reviews
> - Prizes, Sweepstakes and Lotteries
> - Tax Preparers
> - Telephone and Mobile Services
> - Travel, Vacations and Timeshare Plans
>
> **Identity Theft**
> - Bank account
> - Credit Card

panel, Fletcher (2024) included Miscellaneous Reports and Unspecified Reports—as well as the Privacy, Data Security, and Cyber Threat report category (through which the FTC receives some reports and complaints about general cybercrime)—as types of fraud, identifying 47 subcategories. This fluidity is meant to keep FTC's taxonomy of report types as an evolving system, with categories and subcategories created and collapsed over time based on the data being reported and permitting focus on emerging areas/issues of interest. Fletcher (2024) noted that categorization based on the type of good or service at issue avoids the definition of categories based on demographics, contact methods, and monetary loss—so, for instance, reports are not classified as "elder fraud," "phone scams," or "high-loss fraud"; however, that information is collected in the data series, which generally enables distinguishing between cybercrime- and noncybercrime-related instances. The code list of report categories is periodically reviewed; members of the public making reports to the FTC are asked to self-select a category, or one may be assigned by staff (e.g.,

- Employment and/or Tax-Related
- Government Documents or Benefits
- Loan or Lease
- Phone or Utilities
- Other Identity Theft

Other Report Categories
- Auto Related
- Banks and Lenders
- Computer Equipment and Software
- Credit Bureaus, Information Furnishers and Report Users
- Credit Cards and Loss Protection
- Debt Collection
- Education
- Funeral Services
- Home Repair, Improvement and Products
- Privacy, Data Security, and Cyber Threats—"Reports about data privacy, including children's online privacy. This includes reports about the collection, storage, use, disclosure, or disposal of consumer data. Also included are reports about malware and computer exploits, including spyware, malware, denial of service attacks, etc."
- Television and Electronic Media

SOURCE: Consumer Sentinel Network Descriptions of Report Categories, at https://www.ftc.gov/system/files/attachments/data-sets/category_definitions.pdf

through rules-based classification), and the FTC works to crosswalk its classification scheme with those of its data contributors.

Other Entities

Cyber-involved fraud is so ubiquitous and widespread that many other agencies and organizations are working in the field, among them AARP's Fraud Watch Network, the Better Business Bureau, and the Identity Theft Resource Center. For instance, AARP's Fraud Watch Network operates a free helpline, through which all members of the public can report incidents of fraud and receive support from trained volunteers. Reports made through the helpline are sent to the FTC's Consumer Sentinel Network database (described earlier in this chapter). AARP's Fraud Watch Network receives roughly 100,000 reports annually and approximately 300–500 calls per day (Fetterhoff, 2024). In 2024, victim reports to the helpline included identity theft; impostor business; tech support and computer viruses; fraudulent sales; online dating and romance schemes; impostor government schemes; sweepstakes, prize, or lottery schemes; unauthorized money withdrawal; investment fraud and schemes; and phishing (Fetterhoff, 2024). However, the AARP's focus is understandably less on data collection and analysis and more on providing fraud victims with an empathetic ear and necessary information services.

As the U.S. Government Accountability Office (2023) report observed, and as noted by our predecessor Panel on Modernizing the Nation's Crime Statistics, other law enforcement agencies (e.g., Homeland Security Investigations and the U.S. Postal Inspection Service) and information reporting/surveillance systems (e.g., the Financial Crimes Enforcement Network of the U.S. Department of the Treasury) gather information about incidents that may constitute cybercrime, but still operate outside the existing national crime statistics apparatus.

COLLECTION OF CYBERSECURITY INCIDENT INFORMATION AND CYBERCRIME-RELATED INFORMATION FROM BUSINESS AND INDUSTRY

Trusted Entities and Information Sharing Safe-Havens: Information Sharing and Analysis Centers/Organizations and the National Cyber-Forensics and Training Alliance

Information Sharing and Analysis Centers (ISACs) and Information Sharing and Analysis Organizations (ISAOs) are nonprofit organizations intended to serve as trusted entities for information sharing on cybersecurity and cyberthreats. ISACs are public-private partnerships that began to form after issuance of Presidential Decision Directive/NSC-63 in May 1998,[18] which tapped agencies to designate sector coordinators in each of several critical infrastructure sectors to examine and address vulnerabilities to cyberattack. The term ISAO was formally defined in the Homeland Security Act of 2002 (P.L. 107-296; 116 Stat. 2151). ISACs are specific to business/industry sectors falling under the general heading of critical infrastructure, while ISAOs are more flexible in their membership (i.e., they include nonprofit organizations or government agencies) and subject-matter focus area. As of the most current listing, 27 member ISACs (e.g., the Aviation ISAC, Emergency Management and Response ISAC, and Financial Services ISAC) voluntarily contribute to a National Council of ISACs that serves as an operational and coordinating arm across the sectors,[19] while Executive Order 13691 (February 13, 2015) authorized the creation of the

---

[18] See https://clinton.presidentiallibraries.us/items/show/12762
[19] See https://www.nationalisacs.org/members

ISAO Standards Organization to develop similar coordinating resources for the ISAOs.[20]

Through real-time information sharing on cybersecurity incidents and vulnerabilities as well as best practices for countering them, ISACs and ISAOs promote collaboration in hardening defenses against cyberthreats. Threat information is typically reported to ISACs or ISAOs through both formal channels (e.g., automated threat-sharing systems) and informational channels (e.g., direct communication), which ISACs then analyze (typically in anonymized form) and return to member organizations as actionable alerts or guidance. In this work, ISACs frequently interact with the Cybersecurity & Infrastructure Security Agency (CISA) of the USDHS.

The National Cyber-Forensics and Training Alliance (NCFTA) performs a similar function, more formally adding domestic and international law enforcement to the mix. Founded in Pittsburgh in 2002, the NCFTA physically co-locates representatives from private industry and law enforcement with a dedicated team of analysts, with the dual intent of fostering a trusted and neutral environment for collaboration and developing strategies for mitigating and disrupting cybercrime threats (LaVigna, 2024). In a sense, the NCFTA is a model for incentivizing information sharing and collaboration across businesses and organizations, where the incentive is actionable intelligence and realized solutions for major cyberthreats.

Collectively, for purposes of this study, ISACs, ISAOs, and the NCFTA provide useful examples for promoting a culture of information sharing and data sharing within safe havens, across industry and government—even if publication of data products is not part of their current role.

Verizon Data Breach Investigations Reports

The Verizon Data Breach Investigations Report (DBIR) is an annual report series, compiled since 2008 by Verizon Business and its Verizon Threat Research Advisory Center team, based on voluntary submission of cybersecurity incident data from an evolving set of contributors. Data are contributed in or converted to a specific coding schema known as the Vocabulary for Event Recording and Incident Sharing (VERIS); data analyses are made public in the DBIR but the raw data are not, though a VERIS Community Database is an open, publicly available compilation of data breach incidents that have been publicly disclosed.[21] The 2024 edition of the DBIR lists approximately 80 contributing organizations and entities,

---

[20] In October 2015, the University of Texas at San Antonio (in partnership with the Logistics Management Institute and the Retail Cyber Intelligence Sharing Center) was selected to serve as the ISAO Standards Organization; see https://www.isao.org/about/history/

[21] See http://verisframework.org/vcdb

including the FBI IC3, NCFTA, the U.S. Secret Service, CISA, and the public VERIS Community Database, and includes analysis of 30,458 cybersecurity incidents, "of which 10,626 were confirmed data breaches [with] victims spanning 94 countries" (Verizon Business, 2024, p. 5). VERIS is premised on the definition of an incident as "a series of events that adversely affects the information assets of an organization."[22] Accordingly, assets are the first of what VERIS describes as the "4 A's" that combine to characterize a cybersecurity incident:

- *Assets* are the system and network components affected in the incident, with variables identifying the asset's variety (e.g., specific categories of servers, networks, devices, and people), ownership, management, hosting, and accessibility;
- *Attributes* are the security attributes of the asset affected in the incident, which VERIS groups into three paired categories—confidentiality/possession, integrity/authenticity, and availability/utility;
- *Actors* are the "offenders" in the incidents whose actions affected the asset, with many subcategories under the general headings of external (to the organization) actors, internal actors, and partner actors; and
- *Actions* are the specific behaviors and operations that affected the asset.

The list of threat Actions is the closest analogue to a cybercrime offense list in VERIS, and the varieties of Actions defined in VERIS are enumerated in Box 2-8. Each of the seven main varieties—Malware, Hacking, Social Engineering, Misuse of Assets, Physical Actions, Error (Human or Technological), and Environmental—generally includes a list of vectors by which the action was perpetrated (e.g., email attachment or direct install for malware, physical access or web application for hacking). VERIS Actions include two varieties that are pointedly not cybercrime related (i.e., Error, Human or Technological, and Environmental) but five that are highly relevant (i.e., Malware, Hacking, Social Engineering, Misuse of Assets, and Physical Actions).

EMERGING COLLECTIONS OF CYBERSECURITY AND CYBERCRIME-RELATED INCIDENTS

As fragmented as crime statistics data collection is, the situation is arguably even more complicated in the arena of general cybersecurity.

---

[22] See http://verisframework.org/incident-desc.html

BOX 2-8
Covered Threat Actions in the Vocabulary for Event Recording and Incident Sharing Framework

Malware, defined as "any malicious software, script, or code run on a device that alters its state or function without the owner's informed consent"
- *Specific Varieties:* Adware; Backdoor; Brute force; Capture app data; Capture stored data; Client-side attack; Click fraud/Bitcoin mining; Command and control (C2); Destroy data; Disable controls; Denial-of-Service attack; Downloader; Exploit vulnerability in code (vs. misconfiguration or weakness); Export data; Packet sniffer; Password dumper; RAM scraper/memory parser; Ransomware; Rootkit; Scan network; Spam; Spyware/Keylogger; SQL injection; Adminware; Worm; Unknown; Other

Hacking, defined as "all attempts to intentionally access or harm information assets without (or exceeding) authorization by circumventing or thwarting logical security mechanisms"
- *Specific Varieties:* Abuse of functionality; Brute force/password guessing; Buffer overflow; Cache poisoning; Session prediction; Cross-site request forgery; Cross-site scripting; Cryptanalysis; Denial of Service; Footprinting and fingerprinting; Forced browsing or predictable resource location; Format string attack; Fuzz testing; HTTP request smuggling; HTTP request splitting; Integer overflows; LDAP injection; Mail command injection; Man-in-the-middle attack; Null byte injection; Offline cracking; OS commanding; Path traversal; Remote file inclusion; Reverse engineering; Router detour; Session fixation; Session replay; Soap array abuser; Special election injection; SQL injection; SSI injection; URL redirector abuse; Use of backdoor or C2; Use of stolen credentials; XML attributable blowup; XML entity expansion; XML external entities; XML injection; XPath injection; XQuery injection; Virtual machine escape; Unknown; Other

Social Engineering, defined as "tactics [that] employ deception, manipulation, intimidation, etc. to exploit the human element, or users, of information assets"
- *Specific Varieties:* Baiting; Bribery; Elicitation; Extortion; Forgery; Influence; Scam; Phishing; Pretexting; Propaganda/disinformation; Spam; Unknown; Other

Misuse of Assets, defined as "the use of entrusted organizational resources or privileges for any purpose or manner contrary to that which was intended. Includes administrative abuse, use policy violations, use of non-approved assets, etc."; differentiated from Hacking in that misuse actors were legitimately granted access and used it inappropriately (access in Hacking is obtained illegitimately)
- *Specific Varieties*: Knowledge abuse; Privilege abuse; Embezzlement; Data mishandling; Email misuse; Net misuse; Illicit content; Unapproved workaround; Unapproved hardware; Unapproved software; Uknown; Other

Physical Actions, defined as "deliberate threats that involve proximity, possession, or force"
- *Specific Varieties*: Assault; Sabotage; Snooping; Surveillance; Tampering; Theft; Wiretapping; Unknown; Other

continued

> **BOX 2-8 Continued**
>
> **Error (Human or Technological)**, "broadly encompass[ing] anything done (or left undone) incorrectly or inadvertently; it does *NOT* include something done (or left undone) intentionally or by default that later proves to be unwise or inadequate"
> - *Specific Varieties*: Classification error; Data entry error; Disposal error; Gaffe; Loss; Maintenance error; Misconfiguration; Misdelivery; Misinformation; Omission; Physical accidents; Capacity shortage; Programming error; Publishing error; Malfunction; Unknown; Other
>
> **Environmental** factors, including "natural events such as earthquakes and floods, [as well as] hazards associated with the immediate environment or infrastructure in which assets are located"
> - *Specific Varieties*: Deterioration; Earthquake; Electromagnetic interference; Electrostatic discharge; Temperature; Fire; Flood; Hazardous material; Humidity; Hurricane; Ice; Landslide; Lightning; Meteorite; Particulates; Pathogen; Power failure; Tornado; Tsunami; Vermin; Volcano; Water leak; Unknown; Other
>
> SOURCES: Extract from list of Action Enumerations at https://verisframework.org/enums.html, with modifications from conversion to list of Incident Types in public-comment draft of CISA Incident Reporting Form (Appendix 3 in regulations.gov docket CISA 2024-0025-0002).

When major computer security incidents occur—events that may or may not constitute cybercrime but nonetheless pose a threat to commerce and well-being—in government, business, and industry, a daunting and duplicative set of reporting requirements is triggered. In September 2023, the Cyber Incident Reporting Council (CIRC), established by the USDHS, issued its report Harmonization of Cyber Incident Reporting to the Federal Government (U.S. Department of Homeland Security, 2023) (hereafter, the Harmonization report). The report identified at least 45 federal cyber-incident reporting requirements currently enforced by 22 agencies, along with 7 proposed requirements still under development. Notably, one of these seven emerging incident reporting regimes is mandated by the same law—the Cyber Incident Reporting for Critical Infrastructure Act of 2022 (CIRCIA), discussed further in this section—that mandated the creation of the CIRC and the Harmonization report itself.

Untangling and understanding these reporting requirements is a difficult task. For example, the Harmonization report notes that businesses in the financial services sector alone face reporting requirements from eight agencies—the Commodity Futures Trading Commission, the Federal

Deposit Insurance Corporation, the Federal Housing Finance Agency, the Federal Reserve Board, the Financial Crimes Enforcement Network of the U.S. Department of the Treasury, the National Credit Union Administration, the Office of the Comptroller of the Currency, and the Securities and Exchange Commission (SEC)—that vary in their application to businesses in the sector and in the required timeline for reporting. Issues raised concerning cyberincident reporting and the CIRC's suggestions to resolve them are similar to the cybercrime reporting challenges detailed in the U.S. Government Accountability Office (2023) report on cybercrime. The report clearly distinguishes between possible redundancy in the mechanics of *reporting* incidents and simply deeming the multiple reporting *requirements* as duplicative; the reporting itself can be standardized and streamlined to some extent, but the requirements may serve equally legitimate information needs and other important purposes. The Harmonization report calls for development of a standardized set of definitions (in particular, of what constitutes a reportable cyberincident), timelines, and reporting triggers, and suggests model language for each. The report also suggests the creation of a unified reporting portal and development of information sharing protocols to distribute timely and actionable data to the appropriate agencies.

Cybersecurity & Infrastructure Security Agency and the Cyber Incident Reporting for Critical Infrastructure Act

At present, the CISA gathers voluntary reports from businesses, organizations, and the public on cybersecurity incidents under the authority granted it as the designated federal information security incident center by the Federal Information Security Modernization Act of 2014 (FISMA; P.L. 113-283). FISMA defines a reportable "incident" as "an occurrence that—(A) actually or imminently jeopardizes, without lawful authority, the integrity, confidentiality, or availability of information or an information system; or (B) constitutes a violation or imminent threat of violation of law, security policies, security procedures, or acceptable use policies" (44 U.S.C. § 3552), thus encompassing both cybercrime and noncybercrime.

Enacted into law on March 15, 2022, CIRCIA (P.L. 117-103,[23] with technical amendments in P.L. 117-263 [December 23, 2022]; codified at 6 U.S.C. 681–681g) authorized CISA to implement a system for mandatory reporting of cyberincidents by businesses in 16 critical infrastructure

---

[23] Specifically, CIRCIA is Division Y of P.L. 117-103, the broader Consolidated Appropriations Act, 2022, that provided appropriations for nearly all federal agencies for fiscal year 2022. The Violence Against Women Act Reauthorization Act of 2022 that partially motivates this study is Division W of the same appropriations act.

sectors.[24] The CIRCIA act required the CISA to issue a notice of proposed rulemaking (NPRM), which it did in a Federal Register notice dated April 4, 2024 (U.S. Department of Homeland Security, 2024), and to publish the final rule within 18 months of the NPRM (meaning that the final rule is expected in late 2025, and mandatory CIRCIA reporting is slated to begin in 2026).[25]

The CIRCIA NPRM applies mandatory reporting requirements to "covered entities," which refers to businesses in 16 sectors designated by the federal government as critical infrastructure; sector-specific criteria govern inclusion under the rule, though businesses that exceed the small business size standard for a particular industry are automatically covered. The NPRM defines a "cyber incident" as "an occurrence that actually jeopardizes, without lawful authority, the integrity, confidentiality, or availability of information on an information system; or actually jeopardizes, without lawful authority, an information system" (89 F.R. 23766).[26] The CIRCIA NPRM then defines a "substantial cyber incident" as (89 F.R. 23767)

> a cyber incident that leads to any of the following: (1) A substantial loss of confidentiality, integrity or availability of a covered entity's information system or network; (2) A serious impact on the safety and resiliency of a covered entity's operational systems and processes; (3) A disruption of a covered entity's ability to engage in business or industrial operations, or deliver goods or services; (4) Unauthorized access to a covered entity's information system or network, or any nonpublic information contained therein, that is facilitated through or caused by a: (i) Compromise of a cloud service provider, managed service provider, or other third-party data hosting provider; or (ii) Supply chain compromise.

The definition explicitly excludes "the threat of disruption as extortion" (i.e., the mere threat of disruption does not qualify as a ransomware

---

[24] The critical infrastructure sectors are chemical; commercial facilities; communications; critical manufacturing; dams; defense industrial base; emergency services; energy; financial services; food and agriculture; government facilities; healthcare and public health; information technology; nuclear reactors, materials, and waste; transportation systems; and water and wastewater systems.

[25] The acronym "CIRCIA" has come to refer to both the emerging incident reporting system and the law that directed its creation. Hence, even though the usage is redundant with keywords in the acronym, we hereafter speak of the "CIRCIA act" as the text of the law, of the "CIRCIA NPRM" as the draft rule for public comment, and of "CIRCIA reporting" as the objective of the new system.

[26] In this definition, the CIRCIA NPRM preserves the CIRCIA act's sharp distinction between "imminent" and "actual" jeopardy; the act's definition of "cyber incident" explicitly "does not include an occurrence that imminently, but not actually, jeopardizes" an information system or the information contained therein (136 Stat. 1039).

incident) as well as events that are lawfully authorized (e.g., conducted pursuant to a warrant) or executed at the direct request of the owner or operator of the affected system (89 F.R. 23767).[27] Rounding out the fundamental definitions, a "covered cyber incident" is a "substantial cyber incident experienced by a covered entity" (89 F.R. 23766).

Subject to certain exceptions spelled out in detail, the basic timelines of mandatory CIRCIA reporting are exactly those detailed in Section 2242 of the CIRCIA act itself: "a covered entity that experiences a covered cyber incident shall report the covered cyber incident to [CISA] not later than 72 hours after the covered entity reasonably believes that the covered cyber incident has occurred,"[28] and "a covered entity that makes a ransom payment as the result of a ransomware attack against the covered entity shall report the payment to [CISA] not later than 24 hours after the random payment has been made" regardless of whether the ransomware attack itself qualifies as a "covered cyber incident" (136 Stat. 1043).

CIRCIA's emphasis on gathering information on ransomware payments and incidents is not surprising, given that the CIRCIA act took shape in the wake of the May 2021 ransomware attack on the Colonial Pipeline that sparked panic fuel buying and fuel shortages. Moreover, the information that the CISA intends to collect in CIRCIA reporting is extensive and daunting. The draft CIRCIA NPRM specification of minimum information content for an initial report of a covered cyberincident is

---

[27] Two aspects of these definitions are worthy of note. First, from the perspective of potential cybercrime measurement, basic unauthorized access/trespass (except under the conditions of clause (4) of the substantial cyber incident definition) and attempted-but-not-completed breaches and attacks would typically qualify as cybercrime but—in and of themselves—do not appear to qualify for mandatory CIRCIA reporting. Second, the definition differs from (and is generally more narrow than) the model definition of a "reportable cyber incident" set out by the USDHS Harmonization report (U.S. Department of Homeland Security, 2023, p. 26):

> A reportable cyber incident is a cyber incident that leads to, or, if still under the covered entity's investigation, could reasonably lead to any of the following: (1) a substantial loss of confidentiality, integrity, or availability of a covered information system, network, or operational technology; (2) a disruption or significant adverse impact on the covered entity's ability to engage in business operations or deliver goods, or services, including those that have a potential for significant impact on public health or safety or may cause serious injury or death; (3) disclosure or unauthorized access directly or indirectly to non-public personal information of a significant number of individuals; or (4) potential operational disruption to other critical infrastructure systems or assets.

[28] The 72-hour benchmark is also suggested as the model timeline by the USDHS Harmonization report (U.S. Department of Homeland Security, 2023, p. 28), which notes that agencies can and should continue to require incident reports in less than 72 hours (e.g., when potential threat to national security or public safety is especially high, as with transportation operational systems). The model definition provides for the option of a longer-than-72-hour window in "incidents that involve the loss of personal information without further impact on business operations" and the potential harm is relatively slight.

shown in Box 2-9 and spans 10 main items, including potentially sensitive information on vulnerabilities exploited in the attack and the security measures in place; the CIRCIA NPRM's minimum specification for a Ransomware Payment Report is an even longer 14-item list, and a separate passage (Section 226.13) of the draft rule lists 10 broad categories of system log data and other forensic data and records that must be retained in connection with reported incidents. Despite this detail and the clearly defined focus on ransomware, it is difficult to discern something akin to a list of possible reportable events that might map to a cybercrime offense list. The information items in Box 2-9 suggest that cybercrimes such as unauthorized access and deployment of malware are possible elements of a CIRCIA incident, on which detailed information is required to be collected, but the exact manner in which that information will be collected and coded is unclear. Separately, in October 2024, CISA submitted revised versions of its existing reporting forms for review by the U.S. Office of Management and Budget's Office of Information and Regulatory Affairs, pursuant to the terms of the Paperwork Reduction Act,[29] and the draft question list adopts the VERIS framework's list of actions (see Box 2-8) to describe events. However, in filing the revised reporting forms for review, CISA emphasized that these forms are entirely distinct from CIRCIA reporting, for which a new and separate web-based form will be created.

Mandatory Cyberincident Reporting to the Securities and Exchange Commission

In August 2023, the SEC issued a new final rule on "Cybersecurity Risk Management, Strategy, Governance, and Incident Disclosure" (Securities and Exchange Commission, 2023) that adds "material cybersecurity incidents" to the significant events that require public disclosure by publicly traded companies using Form 8-K. Form 8-K filings have traditionally been required for major events in the conduct of business—such as leadership changes, acquisitions, or sales—that may impact a company's market value. Prior to this rule, cybersecurity incidents were often inconsistently reported across different forms, leading to gaps in transparency. The new rule mandates that material cybersecurity incidents be reported to the SEC within four business days[30] of the incident being deemed material—a threshold that differs from the CIRCIA's requirement for critical infrastructure sectors

---

[29] See https://www.reginfo.gov/public/do/PRAViewICR?ref_nbr=202307-1670-004, corresponding to Information Collection Review Reference Number 202307-1670-004, CISA Reporting Forms, and the associated docket for the CISA Incident Reporting Form, at https://www.regulations.gov/docket/CISA-2024-0025

[30] The rule allows for delays in filing if the U.S. Attorney General determines that immediate disclosure would pose a substantial risk to national security or public safety (88 F.R. 51899).

> **BOX 2-9**
> **Required Information for Covered Cyberincident Reports under the Cyber Incident Reporting for Critical Infrastructure Act**
>
> A covered entity must provide all the [previously specified company-identifying information] and the following information in a Covered Cyber Incident Report, to the extent such information is available and applicable to the covered cyber incident:
> (a) A description of the covered cyber incident, including but not limited to:
>   (1) Identification and description of the function of the affected networks, devices, and/or information systems that were, or are reasonably believed to have been, affected by the covered cyber incident, including but not limited to: (i) Technical details and physical locations of such networks, devices, and/or information systems; and (ii) Whether any such information system, network, and/or device supports any elements of the intelligence community or contains [sensitive national defense information];
>   (2) A description of any unauthorized access, regardless of whether the covered cyber incident involved an attributed or unattributed cyber intrusion, identification of any informational impacts or information compromise, and any network location where activity was observed;
>   (3) Dates pertaining to the covered cyber incident, including but not limited to: (i) The date the covered cyber incident was detected; (ii) The date the covered cyber incident began; (iii) If fully mitigated and resolved at the time of reporting, the date the covered cyber incident ended; (iv) The timeline of compromised system communications with other systems; and (v) For covered cyber incidents involving unauthorized access, the suspected duration of the unauthorized access prior to detection and reporting; and
>   (4) The impact of the covered cyber incident on the covered entity's operations, such as information related to the level of operational impact and direct economic impacts to operations; any specific or suspected physical or informational impacts; and information to enable CISA's assessment of any known impacts to national security or public health and safety;
> (b) The category or categories of any information that was, or is reasonably believed to have been, accessed or acquired by an unauthorized person or persons;
> (c) A description of any vulnerabilities exploited, including but not limited to the specific products or technologies and versions of the products or technologies in which the vulnerabilities were found;
> (d) A description of the covered entity's security defenses in place, including but not limited to any controls or measures that resulted in the detection or mitigation of the incident;
>
> *continued*

BOX 2-9 Continued

(e) A description of the type of incident and the tactics, techniques, and procedures used to perpetrate the covered cyber incident, including but not limited to any tactics, techniques, and procedures used to gain initial access to the covered entity's information systems, escalate privileges, or move laterally, if applicable;

(f) Any indicators of compromise, including but not limited to those [specified in required content of Supplemental Reports], observed in connection with the covered cyber incident;

(g) A description and, if possessed by the covered entity, a copy or samples of any malicious software the covered entity believes is connected with the covered cyber incident;

(h) Any identifying information, including but not limited to all available contact information, for each actor reasonably believed by the covered entity to be responsible for the covered cyber incident;

(i) A description of any mitigation and response activities taken by the covered entity in response to the covered cyber incident, including but not limited to:
  (1) Identification of the current phase of the covered entity's incident response efforts at the time of reporting;
  (2) The covered entity's assessment of the effectiveness of response efforts in mitigating and responding to the covered cyber incident;
  (3) Identification of any law enforcement agency that is engaged in responding to the covered cyber incident, including but not limited to information about any specific law enforcement official or point of contact, notifications received from law enforcement, and any law enforcement agency that the covered entity otherwise believes may be involved in investigating the covered cyber incident; and
  (4) Whether the covered entity requested assistance from another entity in responding to the covered cyber incident and, if so, the identity of each entity and a description of the type of assistance requested or received from each entity;

(j) Any other data or information as required by the web-based CIRCIA Incident Reporting Form or any other manner and form of reporting authorized under [the rule].

SOURCE: Excerpted from Section 226.8 of draft rule in U.S. Department of Homeland Security (2024); 89 F.R. 23770–23771.

to report significant cyberincidents to CISA within 72 hours and ransomware payments within 24 hours.

The rule further requires companies to describe their processes for assessing and managing cybersecurity risks, as well as to disclose the roles of management and the board of directors in overseeing these risks.

Both the requirement to file Form 8-K and the timing of such reports depend on the determination of whether a cyberincident is "material." While the rule does not provide specific guidance on how to determine materiality, it relies on the SEC's established practice, supported by case law, that information is material if a reasonable investor would consider it important in making investment decisions. The SEC's definition of "cybersecurity incident" is general in nature—"an unauthorized occurrence, or a series of related unauthorized occurrences, on or conducted through a registrant's information systems that jeopardizes the confidentiality, integrity, or availability of a registrant's information systems or any information residing therein"—and thus seems to include both incidents that are recognizable as cybercrimes and incidents that are not.

Another important difference between the new SEC Form 8-K requirements and the emerging CIRCIA reporting, noted by the SEC rule, is the intended role of the information disclosure. Though the CIRCIA permits and expects that incidents reported to CISA may be shared with law enforcement entities, in the interest of coordinating all-of-government response to emerging threats and deterring future cyberattacks, the data are otherwise meant to be confidential disclosures. However, in the SEC context, public (and investor/stakeholder) awareness is the main impetus; disclosures are intended to get information (e.g., on major cybersecurity incidents) to public investors in a timely manner, so that they are aware of risks that may impact the company's performance.

INTERNATIONAL PARALLELS: CYBERCRIME DATA COLLECTION IN CANADA

Collection of crime statistics in Canada is coordinated by the Canadian Centre for Justice and Community Safety Statistics (CCJCSS), a program within Statistics Canada. The primary vehicle, analogous to the U.S. UCR Program, is also branded UCR but is known as the Uniform Crime Reporting Survey. Under Canadian law, the Royal Canadian Mounted Police and every police service in Canada are required to report crime data to the CCJCSS; the system has developed into monthly extracts directly from police records management systems (RMS), with various iterations of the UCR Survey being incorporated into the RMS technical specifications.

Version 2.2 of the UCR Survey, introduced in 2004, added a two-field Cyber Crime variable to the data collection, based on the general definition of cybercrime as "a criminal offence involving a computer as the object of the crime or the tool used to commit a material component of the offence" (Canadian Centre for Justice Statistics, Policing Services Program, 2008, p. 61). The first field asked whether the incident involved a cybercrime under this definition (Yes, No, or Unknown as to whether the incident involved a computer or the internet). If the answer in the first field was "Yes," the second field delineated two broad categories for the cybercrime type as well as an "Unknown" response option (Canadian Centre for Justice Statistics, Policing Services Program, 2008, p. 62):

- *Target*, meaning that "a computer or the internet is the target of the crime," thus including offenses such as "computer hacking, defacing websites and unauthorized use of computer systems"; and
- *Instrument*, meaning that "computers or the Internet are tools used to commit the crime," as in "distribution/sale of child pornography over the Internet, criminal harassment via emails, or fraud perpetrated over the Internet."

Sauvé and Silver (2024, p. 10) note that the UCR Survey evolved the description of the Cyber Crime variable to reference ICT generally, where "ICT includes, but is not limited to, the internet, computers, servers, digital technology, digital telecommunications devices, phones and networks."

In Version 2.4 of the UCR Survey, which took effect in 2021 and began full implementation in spring 2024, the cybercrime type indicator was substantially revised and replaced with a new classification variable. The revision drew from the creation of a Cyber Classification Compendium (CCC), an attempt to create a crosswalk between cybercrime offense types and definitions in international and U.S. law (Wright & Parker, 2023). As discussed further in Chapter 3, the CCC partitions cybercrime into nine broad categories: Malware; System and Service Availability; Information Gathering; Intrusion; Data Release (information security compromise); Frauds; Abusive Content; Exploitation, Harassment, or Abuse of a Person; and Uncategorized (Wright, 2024; Wright & Parker, 2023). Because full implementation began only recently, it is not yet known how effective the variable has been in practice.

3

Approaches to Cybercrime Classification

For purposes of our study of cybercrime classification and measurement, Chapter 2's review of the handling of cybercrime definitions in current crime statistics and current cybercrime/cybersecurity measures affirms that there is no universally agreed-upon definition of cybercrime and its types. To the extent that current data collections follow a taxonomy of cybercrime, it is a taxonomy only in the sense of being a list, otherwise lacking organizational principles in its construction. This is not to disparage the existing collections; there are admirable aspects to the effectively data-defined nature of the Internet Crime Complaint Center's code list, for example, where entries shuffle on or off the list—or are split or combined as appropriate—based on their observed frequency.

Our fundamental task was to review current data collections and organizational schema to suggest a better approach, which is described in this chapter. We first identify previous attempts to define a rigorous taxonomy for cybercrime in its own right as well as to nest cybercrime in the context of crime writ large. Based on this review and our observations of the current data-collection systems, we define a set of desired principles for our classification and then outline our suggested taxonomy.

CYBER-SPECIFIC TAXONOMIES: CYBERCRIME IN ISOLATION

Our review of the partitioning and classification of cybercrime in stand-alone taxonomies owes greatly to the comprehensive literature review of Phillips et al. (2022) as well as their proposed classification schema, which was subsequently summarized along with other schema in the Brinton et al.

(2023) "environmental scan" of cybercrime measurement to inform options for cybercrime content in the National Crime Victimization Survey (NCVS).

Arguably the most common dimension along which cybercrime offenses are divided in proposed taxonomies—including the language of our panel's statement of task—is the degree of cyber or computer involvement. Phillips et al. (2022) attribute a basic two-way split between cyber-enabled and cyber-dependent crime to an original definition advanced by Brenner (2007) and a three-way split that adds cyber-assisted crime to Wall (2005). In the Phillips et al. (2022, p. 385) rendition of the Wall (2005) taxonomy, the basic categories are as follows:

- Cyber-dependent crime/pure cybercrime, in which cyber/computer involvement is absolutely essential to the offense, which could not have occurred without it; this includes hacking, ransomware, and malware deployment.
- Cyber-enabled crime/hybrid cybercrime, in which cyber/computer involvement facilitates the offense or makes it easier to perpetrate, but the offense could ultimately have been accomplished by other means; this includes fraud and the dissemination of child sexual abuse material.
- Cyber-assisted crime/computer-assisted traditional crime, in which the cyber involvement is incidental to a real/physical–world crime; this includes criminal communications or the use of information and communication technology (ICT) to lure a victim into a physical attack.

Phillips et al. (2022, p. 384) attribute to Wall (2007) a related dimension along which cybercrime might be split—namely, the role of "the machine" in the offense:

- Crimes against the machine, or computer integrity crimes (akin to cyber-dependent crime);
- Crimes using the machine, combining various computer-assisted or computer-enabled crimes such as fraud; and
- Crimes in the machine, or computer content/content-related crimes, in which the cyber/computer involvement is the necessary communication conduit (e.g., for online dissemination of child sexual abuse material or online hate incitement).

Statistics Canada rolls cybercrimes into a similar two-level split between ICT being either the target of the offense or the instrument of the offense (Sauvé & Silver, 2024).

Brenner (2004) suggests a breakdown of cybercrimes by the extent of harm—individual harm, systemic harm, and inchoate harm—that evokes the very loose categorization of offenses in the National Incident-Based Reporting System (NIBRS; discussed later in this chapter) as crimes against individuals, society, or property. Gordon and Ford (2006, p. 13) propose a distinction between Type I and Type II cybercrime; the former is "mostly technological" in nature while the latter "has a more pronounced human element." More commonly, though, proposed cybercrime taxonomies work to distill some set of fundamental nature-of-harm groupings:

- One of the earliest proposed cybercrime taxonomies (Wall, 2001) designated Cyber-Trespass, Cyber-Deception/Theft, Cyber-Pornography and Obscenity, and Cyber-Violence as its fundamental offenses.
- Marcum and Higgins (2019) denote five basic categories: Cyberbullying and Cyberstalking, Digital Piracy, Hacking and Malware, Identity Theft, and Sex-Related Crimes Online (further subdividing cyberbullying into five types and hacking/malware into six types).
- The CCC (Wright & Parker, 2023) described in Chapter 2, which is the basis for new cybercrime data collection in Canadian police-report statistics, identifies nine top-level categories as basic offenses—Malware; System and Service Availability; Information Gathering; Intrusion; Data Release (information security compromise); Frauds; Abusive Content; Exploitation, Harassment, or Abuse of a Person; and Uncategorized (Wright, 2024; Wright & Parker, 2023).

Finally, in the context of cybercrime-specific taxonomies, it is instructive to examine how cybercrime types are defined in international law, namely by the Budapest Convention on Cybercrime of 2001 (Council of Europe, 2001) and by the draft United Nations (UN) Convention on Cybercrime (United Nations, 2024), which cleared critical committee votes in August 2024 and was adopted by the General Assembly on December 24, 2024.[1] High-level categories of both treaty instruments are depicted in Box 3-1. Core nature-of-harm categories—illegal access, interception, and interference—are shared between the two treaty documents, with the 2024 UN convention adopting more modern nomenclature (e.g., ICT rather than computer systems) and taking a particularly strong stance against child sexual abuse material, as well as adding the distinctly cyber-enabled offense of laundering proceeds of crime.

---

[1] See https://www.unodc.org/unodc/en/cybercrime/convention/home.html

> **BOX 3-1**
> **Basic Cybercrime Types Identified in the**
> **Budapest Convention on Cybercrime (2001)**
> **and the Draft United Nations Convention**
> **on Cybercrime (August 2024)**
>
> **Budapest Convention on Cybercrime**
> - Offences against the confidentiality, integrity and availability of computer data and systems
>   - Illegal access
>   - Illegal interception
>   - Data interference
>   - System interference
>   - Misuse of devices
> - Computer-related offences
>   - Computer-related forgery
>   - Computer-related fraud
> - Content-related offences
>   - Offences related to child pornography
>   - Offences related to infringements of copyright and related rights
>
> *Also includes articles on attempt/aiding/abetting, corporate liability, and sanctions and measures*
>
> **Cybercrime (Draft August 2024)**
> - Illegal access [of an information and communications technology (ICT) system]
> - Illegal interception [of electronic data]
> - Interference with electronic data

CYBERCRIME IN CONTEXT OF ALL-CRIME TAXONOMIES

Chapter 2 and Appendix C provide considerable detail on how cybercrime content was incorporated into the NIBRS over time. Though the NIBRS offense code list (Table 2-1) does not have the rigorous structure of a fully developed classification scheme, the NIBRS is still the essential reference point for this study, so it is useful to recap highlights of the NIBRS's handling of cybercrime matters. From the outset, NIBRS contributors were guided to code computer-related crimes as the closest underlying base crime in the NIBRS set (e.g., Fraud or Extortion), with Data Element 8 (Offender Suspected of Using [Computer Equipment]) available to mark the added context. When a concerted effort was made to increase cybercrime content, the Federal Bureau of Investigation added one purely computer-centric offense type (Hacking/Computer Invasion)

APPROACHES TO CYBERCRIME CLASSIFICATION 81

- Interference with an ICT system
- Misuse of devices
- ICT system-related forgery
- ICT system-related theft or fraud
- Offences related to online child sexual abuse or child sexual exploitation material
- Solicitation or grooming for the purpose of committing a sexual offence against a child
- Non-consensual dissemination of intimate images
- Laundering of proceeds of crime

Also includes articles on liability of legal persons; participation and attempt; statute of limitations; and prosecution, adjudication, and sanctions

NOTES: Each subcategory is typically accompanied by one or more reservations or declarations that signatory nations may choose to exercise in the ratification process, identifying sections that they decline to add to national law or handle differently. Two additional protocols were added to the Budapest Convention in 2003 and 2022, the 2003 protocol being relevant here as it defined additional offenses for "acts of a racist and xenophobic nature committed through computer systems" (European Treaty Series No. 189). However, the United States was not a signatory to the 2003 protocol and thus has not ratified (it was a signatory to the 2022 protocol on cooperative disclosure of electronic evidence, but has not been ratified). The United Nations Convention on Cybercrime was adopted by the General Assembly on December 24, 2024, and is expected to be opened for member nation ratification in 2025.

SOURCE: Panel generated from Council of Europe (2001) and United Nations (2024).

and one heavily computer-based offense (Identity Theft) to its roster, both with code numbers that positioned them as variants in the broader category of fraud. Cyberspace was also added as a response option to NIBRS Data Element 9, the location of the incident, providing another hook to indicate potential cybercrime involvement.

In the early 2010s, the United Nations Office on Drugs and Crime (2015; UNODC) convened an expert group to construct an International Classification of Crime for Statistical Purposes (ICCS), with the intent of truly covering all crime, touching on areas such as environmental crime that were completely new to traditional crime statistics. The UNODC working group chose to address cybercrime by defining a limited number of what we have just described as cyber-dependent crimes, under the general heading of acts against public safety and state security:

09	Acts against public safety and state security
0903	Acts against computer systems
09031	Unlawful access to a computer system
09032	Unlawful interference with a computer system or computer data
090321	Unlawful interference with a computer system
090322	Unlawful interference with computer data
09033	Unlawful interception or access of computer data
09039	Other acts against computer systems

A critical part of the ICCS design is a system of tags, also termed attributes or disaggregating variables, to provide additional detail or context about the offense. Among the ICCS's disaggregation variables, "Cy" or Cybercrime-related "serves to identify various forms of crime committed with the use of a computer, internet fraud, cyber-stalking or violation of copyright through electronic dissemination" (United Nations Office on Drugs and Crime, 2015, p. 21). The "Cy" tag became the primary mechanism for coding cyber-enabled crime.

Tasked with developing a taxonomy for all types of crime in the American context, our predecessor Panel on Modernizing the Nation's Crime Statistics (hereafter, MNCS panel; National Academies of Sciences, Engineering, and Medicine [National Academies], 2016a, pp. 129–130, 136) maintained the same set of core cyber-dependent crimes—the fundamental offenses of unlawful access, unlawful interference, and unlawful interception—as the ICCS. However, the MNCS panel changed the numbering scheme (e.g., 09 to 5, 0903 to 5.3, and so forth) and shifted the group to the top-level "Acts against property only" category. The MNCS panel also sought to clarify the meaning of the "Cybercrime-related" tag, making it a Yes/No variable "depending on whether the use of computer data or computer systems was an integral part of the modus operandi of the offense." Because of its inclusion in the NIBRS, the MNCS panel also added Identity Theft to its offense tables as number 7.1.2, a disaggregate version of 7 (Acts involving fraud, deception, or corruption) and 7.1 (Fraud). In this way, both the MNCS panel and the ICCS adhere to a definition-plus-attribute structure to allow for the coding of detailed events without explicitly building out dozens of detailed codes and definitions.

Principles and Desired Characteristics of a Taxonomy

As the MNCS panel did in developing its all-crime classification (National Academies, 2016a, pp. 117–124), we settled on a set of principles and desired characteristics in developing our own recommended taxonomy. The current panel's opinion is as follows:

- The taxonomy of cybercrime should satisfy all the requirements of a classification for statistical purposes; namely, it should be exhaustive of the entire space of cybercrime, should partition that space into mutually exclusive categories, and should follow a hierarchical structure to the extent practicable.
- Definitions of cybercrime offenses should be behavioral in nature and focus on the underlying action. As much as possible, the basic definitions should avoid the use of technical jargon and references to specific technologies or computing techniques. In the parlance of the Vocabulary for Event Recording and Incident Sharing (VERIS) described in Chapter 2, the taxonomy's categories should keep Actions distinct from specific reference to the Assets, Actors, and vectors of the attack.[2]
- Relatedly, the number of major categories should be kept as small as possible, and the corresponding offenses should be relatively coarse in construction. This aims to avoid technology-specific jargon and to make the taxonomy easier to interpret and implement. However, this structure also addresses our panel's charge and its principal focus on incorporating the taxonomy into NIBRS and direct reporting from law enforcement agencies—fewer, coarser categories are better suited to data collection in contexts when technical details may not be known or may be impossible to accurately parse and capture in conventional police records management systems.
- As much as possible, definitions in the proposed taxonomy should (a) be consistent with but not strictly limited by the text of state and federal penal codes (because, by definition, crime must be unlawful behavior);and (b) be consistent with existing definitions in major relevant data collections.
- The taxonomy should include both practical, feasible, and (relatively) easily implementable categories, as well as categories that are broader and more aspirational in nature.
- The taxonomy should not be conceived or portrayed as a static, unchanging document; it should be amenable to—and will vitally depend upon—a regular program of monitoring and revision based on findings from resulting data collection.

---

[2] The fourth A in the VERIS framework, Attributes (i.e., the security attributes of the asset affected in the incident), is more difficult to keep distinct from category definitions, as they speak to broader motives for the offending action. See http://verisframework.org/incident-desc.html for further detail on VERIS.

Phillips et al. (2022) combined several dimensions of cybercrime-specific taxonomies in developing their own proposed classification. Their classification framework (Phillips et al., 2022, Figure 1) delineates six main substantive categories—attacks against data and systems, attacks against property or theft, interpersonal violence, sexual violence, violence against groups, and incidental technology use—as well as a more vague violence (general) category and two overarching cross-category bundles of terms. Combining several elements as it does, the Phillips et al. (2022) taxonomy was persuasive as we shaped our own classification. But, for our purposes, it has three key liabilities. First—and understandably, given its genesis in studies of child psychology—it pointedly extends beyond cybercrime and into cyberdeviance, bad behavior that is not necessarily unlawful/criminal. Second, though it effectively pulls many concepts together into one diagram, it stops short of actual definitions for any of its terms. Third, the overarching "violence (general)" and "cross-category" categories are inherently technical violations of the mutual exclusivity criterion we seek for a classification for statistical purposes. That said, the literature review and the proposed classification framework suggested by Phillips et al. (2022) were both valuable contributions to our work.

RECOMMENDED CLASSIFICATION OF CYBERCRIME

The taxonomy we recommend for cybercrime classification and measurement is provided in short form in Recommendation 3-1, expressed graphically in Figure 3-1, and fully articulated with detailed definitions and inclusions in Appendix B.

Recommendation 3-1: The following concise taxonomy should be used as an initial framework for developing statistical measures of cybercrime in the United States:
1 Acts Targeted Against Machines, Data, or Systems
 1A Ransomware
 1B Unlawful Access or Deprivation of Access
 1C Unlawful Interference, Tampering, or Content Release
 1D Other Acts Targeted Against Machines, Data, or Systems
2 Fraud and Acts Targeted Against Property
 2A Identity Theft
 2B Fraud
 2C Other Acts Targeted Against Property
3 Acts Against Individuals, Nonsexual in Nature
4 Acts Against Individuals, Sexual in Nature
5 Acts Targeted Against Groups
6 Acts Involving Incidental Technology Use
NA Acts with No Cyber/Computer Involvement

1 Acts Targeted Against Machines, Data, or Systems	2 Fraud and Acts Targeted Against Property	6 Acts Involving Incidental Technology Use

1A Ransomware
1B Unlawful Access or Deprivation of Access
  e.g., Cybertrespass; denial-of-service attacks
1C Unlawful Interference, Tampering, or Content Release
  e.g., Hacking; destructive malware; unlawful data breach
1D Other Acts Targeted Against Machines, Data, or Systems
	2A Identity Theft
	  Includes elements of both unlawful acquisition of personal information (theft) and misuse of that information to commit fraud (e.g., abuse existing account or create new account)
	2B Fraud
	  e.g., Phishing/social engineering; swindle or confidence game
	2C Other Acts Targeted Against Property
	
	3 Acts Against Individuals, Nonsexual in Nature
	  e.g., Cyberharassment; cyberstalking; cyberbullying
	
	4 Acts Against Individuals, Sexual in Nature
	  e.g., Unlawful sexual exploitation material via electronic means
	
	5 Acts Targeted Against Groups
	  e.g., Computer-related acts of terrorism or radicalization
		e.g., Using information and communication technology to lure a victim into a physical attack

Cyber-dependent; Cyber-enabled; Cyber-assisted;
high cyber/computer involvement moderate cyber/computer involvement low cyber/computer involvement

FIGURE 3-1 Schematic of proposed classification of cybercrime.
SOURCE: Panel generated.

This recommended taxonomy is designed to be exhaustive of the degree of cyber/computer involvement, with main category 1 being pure cyber-dependent crime, categories 2–5 representing more moderate levels of cyberenabling of base crimes, and category 6 representing only incidental cyber/computer involvement (with the final category of Acts with No Cyber/Computer Involvement completing the partitioning). Categories 2–5 are structured by the target of the offense, whether property, individuals, or groups of people. Within major categories 1 and 2, we sparingly delineate specific offenses, preserving Ransomware and Identity Theft as main offenses because of their prominence in public discussion. Category 1B hearkens to the original Wall (2001) designation of "Cyber-Trespass," or simple access, as a fundamental nature of harm in cybercrime, while group 1C pivots to actual damage to computers, networks, or data.

The final shape of this recommended taxonomy resulted from our intention for the classification to be actionable and implementable with or without a massive revision of the classification for all crime. We concur with the MNCS panel that the nation's current crime statistics fall short of capturing information on new, important, and emerging types of crime, and we support the aspirational goal of a next-generation NIBRS that can cover a wider array of offense types. But—in the present—we also recognize the uniquely delicate and challenging climate for crime and cybercrime data collection. Accordingly, our suggestion is to use the recommended taxonomy as an enhanced attribute flag for incidents—one that can be applied regardless of the underlying set of base crimes. We concur with the MNCS panel that much information could be gained by recording events as base offenses plus an attribute flag (in this case, for cyber/computer involvement).

Recommendation 3-2: Rather than have a cybercrime classification function as parallel or adjunct to existing crime classifications, the taxonomy presented in Recommendation 3-1 should be implemented in crime data–collection systems as an attribute, flag, or modifier to code incidents in conjunction with the system's base classification of criminal offenses.

Our Appendix B definitions—developed to apply independently of the base offense list—do not necessarily square completely with the definitions in the current NIBRS or any other particular system. For instance, we define cyberharassment and cyberstalking as examples of offenses that may be included in our category 3, Acts Against Individuals, Nonsexual in Nature. This is consistent with the MNCS panel's formulation, which defines both Harassment and Stalking as course-of-conduct offenses, requiring a demonstrated pattern of activity over a period of time, but it does not comport with the current NIBRS, in which Stalking is listed as an included offense under Intimidation, which is not a course-of-conduct offense, and Harassment is not separately defined at all.

That said, implementing this cybercrime-classification flag in the current NIBRS could fit very well with the current Hacking/Computer Invasion and Identity Theft offenses. The category 1 subdivisions of the taxonomy would provide meaningful disaggregation of the base offense of Hacking/Computer Invasion (pure cyber-dependent crime), while categories 2–5 would shed light on the target of the cybercrime-related instances of other NIBRS base offenses. Meanwhile, Identity Theft is a particularly challenging offense to operationalize because the name implies limitation to theft (i.e., unlawful acquisition of personally identifiable information), but it is traditionally interpreted to include elements of identity fraud (e.g., subsequent use of that personal information to open a new credit card). This two-pronged definition is used by the NCVS Identity Theft Supplement, by NIBRS itself,[3] and by researchers such as Golladay (2020), and we adopt this broader definition in Appendix B, as well. In practice, this means that the ideal way to enter such an offense in NIBRS would be to make use of the system's capacity for associating multiple offenses with the same incident—that is, to include a record with (at least) offenses of Identity Theft and Credit Card Fraud, while selecting the 2A Identity Theft option in our cybercrime-involvement variable.

---

[3]Identity Theft is defined in NIBRS as "wrongfully obtaining and/or using another person's personal data" (Federal Bureau of Investigation, 2023b, p. 27).

4

Recommendations and Implementation Challenges

CALIBRATE EXPECTATIONS: MARKERS OF CYBERCRIME, NOT EXACT MEASUREMENT

We close this report with some guidance on implementation, beginning with a restatement of a fundamental point raised at the outset: while generating reliable national measures of cybercrime is an essential goal and improvements in cybercrime measurement are definitely possible, it is important to approach such improvements with tempered expectations. We raise this point as a respectful but firm push-back against the basic construction of the Better Cybercrime Metrics Act (BCMA; see Appendix A) that occasioned this study. We conclude that cybercrime is too broad a concept and too awkward a match with the concepts and data-collection practices of the existing national crime statistics apparatus to address well by simply "establish[ing] a category in the National Incident-Based Reporting System" (NIBRS) or "includ[ing] questions relating to cybercrime victimization in the National Crime Victimization Survey" (NCVS). Akin to our predecessor Panel on Modernizing the Nation's Crime Statistics (hereafter, MNCS panel; National Academies of Sciences, Engineering, and Medicine [National Academies], 2016a, 2018), we stress our opinion that generation of reliable estimates of cybercrime should be the principal objective—drawing from multiple data sources, each collecting information on offenses and characteristics of offenses according to the source's unique strengths—and that an exact enumeration of cybercrime from any single data resource is infeasible. For instance, the improved cybercrime metrics promised by the BCMA will likely come from a blending of NIBRS and Cyber Incident

Reporting for Critical Infrastructure Act (CIRCIA) reporting to benchmark levels and flows of basic cybercrime types, use of NCVS supplement survey work to illustrate the human dimensions and impact of technology-driven crime, and inference from Internet Crime Complaint Center (IC3) and CIRCIA reporting data to explain the technological story behind the figures and inform responses to the nation's cybercrime problems.

Conclusion 4-1: Improving cybercrime measurement is important, but it is equally important that improvements be made with tempered, realistic expectations of the timing and extent of improvement. Cybercrime is an expansive and evolving topic, so it is unlikely that any single statistical source will effectively cover all of its dimensions; analysts will need to make best use of available information from an array of sources to derive markers of cybercrime activity.

MEASURING CYBERCRIME BY LEVERAGING EXISTING DATA-COLLECTION EFFORTS

National Incident-Based Reporting System

The panel's charge tasked us to focus primarily on the fit of cybercrime into the NIBRS, and we crafted our recommended taxonomy and related guidance with an eye toward successful implementation. We agree with the MNCS panel that the nation would benefit from an extension of the NIBRS to include newer crime types not traditionally handled in police-report statistics, but we also understand that major change can be difficult and expensive. Currently, the NIBRS is establishing itself as a fully operational system; work is ongoing to get all jurisdictions to report—and report effectively—in the new format, and the NIBRS data-provider and data-user communities are still attempting to demonstrate the analytical benefits of the detailed data format. Accordingly, we cast our recommended cybercrime taxonomy as a flag of cybercrime involvement in crime incidents—not requiring a wholesale revision of crime categories up front, though we do support NIBRS's eventual expansion to cover new and as-yet-uncovered crime types. We frame our guidance for the implementation as a series of incremental steps.

In the near term, we recommend steps to assess the current cybercrime-related content in the NIBRS and to establish conditions for successful implementation of the recommended taxonomy:

Recommendation 4-1: The Federal Bureau of Investigation Uniform Crime Reporting Program should consider the following modifications to the existing National Incident-Based Reporting System (NIBRS), preparatory to a more comprehensive cybercrime-collection effort:

1. Continue collecting the existing NIBRS offense categories of Hacking/Computer Invasion and Identity Theft, while actively encouraging participating law enforcement agencies to report these offenses;
2. Clarify the definition and intended role of the two NIBRS data elements that nominally indicate cybercrime involvement, Data Element 8 with Computer Equipment as response to Offender Suspected of Using and Data Element 9 with Cyberspace as response to Location;
3. Consider adding data/systems and digital currency/cryptocurrency as additional intangible property types in Data Element 14 (Type Property Loss/Etc.); and
4. Work with the records management system vendor community to ease NIBRS data entry and improve understanding of new elements, and incorporate information and examples associated with these modifications as part of NIBRS data-provider education and training.

Three important points are embedded in these near-term recommendations. First, we acknowledge that the crime types added in earlier attempts to gain an understanding of cybercrime—Hacking/Computer Invasion and Identity Theft—are a reasonably good starting position. Hacking/Computer Invasion is an adequate initial casting of pure cyber-dependent crime, and our recommended taxonomy-based cybercrime-involvement flag would (through main category 1) provide a breakdown of those offenses by the basic nature of the harm. Identity Theft is slightly more problematic because such incidents need not necessarily involve computer use (and thus are not automatically cybercrime), but Identity Theft has high public salience and breaks the mold of traditional street crime by using identity as an intangible property type. Hence, rather than requiring that Hacking/Computer Invasion and Identity Theft be fundamentally redefined and overhauled up front, the greater imperative is to make data collection for these crime types a stronger norm for the NIBRS.

A second point embedded in this guidance is that implementation of a useful cybercrime-involvement attribute variable will benefit from taking stock of the two existing but fundamentally limited NIBRS data elements that speak to pieces of cybercrime. Data Element 8 has always been an awkwardly constructed variable, fusing response options that indicate whether an offender was believed to be under the influence of mind-altering substances (i.e., the current alcohol and drug response options) with the option of noting use of computer equipment by the offender. The recent redefinition of "Computer Equipment" to "Computer Equipment (Handheld Devices)" seems to make the data element more internally consistent, casting computer involvement as another distraction/"under the influence" dimension (i.e., driving while texting), but does so at the expense of letting the data element serve as a potential marker of cybercrime. Meanwhile, the addition of Cyberspace as a response category for location is useful but also slightly murky. The definition and examples suggest the need for internet involvement and consequently blur differences between the vector by which the attack was perpetrated (i.e., the technological/communications medium used in the offense) and the actual geographic location where the harm was realized. Our recommended taxonomy is meant to provide a more effective cybercrime-involvement indicator and we urge its implementation, but we also note the importance of clarifying the intent and objectives of the existing related data elements first.

A third embedded point is also consistent with the work of the MNCS panel: the notion that data systems like the NIBRS will be most effective when generation of their data submissions is a routine by-product of agencies' day-to-day use of their own records management systems (RMS). As long as the NIBRS requires special, additional processing (particularly by agencies that may lack resources dedicated to the task), obtaining full and accurate participation will be challenging. Hence, we urge the involvement of the RMS vendor community in making NIBRS features and indicators easier to enter accurately.

These near-term, preparatory suggestions are meant to ease the way for fundamental change.

Recommendation 4-2: Following the preparatory steps of Recommendation 4-1, and possibly in conjunction with adoption of a modern classification of crime for statistical purposes, the Federal Bureau of Investigation should incorporate the cybercrime taxonomy in Recommendation 3-1 as a new, mandatory data element in the National Incident-Based Reporting System Incident Segment. Implementing this new data element may involve consolidating or revising existing computer/cyber-related responses in Data Elements 8 and 9.

Though we do not escalate it to the level of a formal recommendation, we present an additional consideration for the future, motivated by the implementation history of the Uniform Crime Reporting (UCR) Program and the NIBRS. State, local, tribal, and territorial law enforcement agencies commonly worry that addition of new crimes and concepts generates spikes in their observed crime rates. This is of particular concern for something like wider coverage of cybercrime, which could increase the number of incidents reported to local law enforcement that are not directly actionable, thus distorting arrest statistics and casting law enforcement work in a negative light. Hence, we suggest that the NIBRS program consider adding an additional clearance code for cybercrime, to clarify that local law enforcement not be held liable for the increased number of unresolved/unresolvable cases on their books.

National Crime Victimization Survey

With respect to the NCVS, our guidance is similar if more pointed in terms of long-term work. The household-survey nature of the NCVS makes it uniquely suited to generate contextual information about crimes and cybercrimes with a distinctly personal effect (e.g., consumer fraud)—and simultaneously makes it ill-suited to assess other crimes with more indirect effects (i.e., unauthorized system access or the other purely cyber-dependent crimes in our recommended taxonomy). Moreover, a critical aspect of the NCVS in illuminating personal-impact cybercrimes is its capacity to suggest explanations about why incidents may not be reported to law enforcement or other authorities. Understandably, the cybercrime types that best match the capabilities of the NCVS—cyber-involved identity theft, fraud, stalking, and harassment—are already the focus of principal NCVS supplemental surveys. Brinton et al. (2023) observe that, with additional research, personal-impact cybercrimes such as phishing/social engineering (as a variant of fraud) and image-based sexual abuse (including cyber-enabled sextortion) might be usefully examined by the NCVS, and we concur—with the proviso that periodic supplements may be the best vehicle for NCVS cybercrime content rather than the core NCVS instrument itself.

> Recommendation 4-3: The Bureau of Justice Statistics should leverage its existing National Crime Victimization Survey supplements with cybercrime-related content (Supplemental Fraud Survey, Identity Theft Supplement, Supplemental Victimization Survey) to contribute to the nation's understanding of cybercrime. This includes refining the content of those supplements as needed as well as working with data users to facilitate analysis and use of the resulting data, including comparison with other data sources.

> Recommendation 4-4: Pending the availability of additional resources for victimization survey work, the Bureau of Justice Statistics should consider increasing the frequency of the three existing cybercrime-related supplements or the fielding of a dedicated cybercrime supplement.

To clarify this point, there are two logical extensions that could be made to include more cybercrime-related content in the core NCVS as opposed to the periodic supplements. The first would be to change the NCVS-2 Crime Incident Report to include relevant content, such as a flag for cyber/computer involvement in the crime. The important limitation of this approach is that to be administered in the NCVS-2 Crime Incident Report, a respondent would still need to indicate the occurrence of a crime type covered in the NCVS. Hence, the follow-up question would provide a relatively narrow look at cyber-enabled or cyber-incidental interpersonal crimes. This limitation suggests a need for the second approach—a much larger expansion that would include cybercrime-related content in the NCVS-1 Basic Screen Questionnaire, thus triggering additional interview cases to collect detailed information with the NCVS-2 Crime Incident Report. At this time, the panel does not recommend adding cybercrime content to the core NCVS instruments, as illustrated by lack of formal mention in Recommendation 4-4, because it is unclear whether the benefit of the information would outweigh the substantial additional resources needed to add the content.

Other Data-Collection Systems

The MNCS panel envisioned improvements to the two current pillars of U.S. crime statistics (i.e., the Federal Bureau of Investigation [FBI]'s UCR and the NCVS) alongside work with "a variety of primarily administrative record-type data sources, primarily for coverage of new crime types that are outside the scope" of the other collection methodologies (National Academies, 2018, p. 39). This multiple-source approach is particularly relevant to cybercrime. Because our charge (and the BCMA that motivated it) is heavily focused on the extant data collections of the NIBRS and NCVS, we do not offer specific recommendations for potential new data-collection systems. However, we do support the approach—we encourage that development of such systems be monitored and studied, so they can eventually play a role in thorough cybercrime measurement. Statistics Canada is beginning to require its constituent law enforcement agencies to report data using a detailed list of cybercrime codes; it is important to examine this work as it progresses, to apply lessons learned to the U.S. NIBRS data collection and training. Similarly, as the release of a final rule approaches and timely reporting of major cybersecurity incidents in important sectors of the U.S. economy and government becomes mandatory, it is important that the CIRCIA collection and similar reporting rules instituted by the Securities and Exchange Commission (SEC) be nurtured and evaluated. The CIRCIA, in particular, is intended to collect information about (and payments made in) ransomware incidents as a major area of focus. Though neither the CIRCIA nor the SEC collection is currently explicitly envisioned as part of the nation's cybercrime data-collection apparatus, the potential is great and, as we discuss later in this chapter, is a critical part of the long-term future of cybercrime measurement.

ASPIRATIONAL GOALS FOR CYBERCRIME MEASUREMENT

Governance and Coordination of National Cybercrime Statistics

In making the case for crime measurement as a system-of-systems, the MNCS panel emphasized that addressing the lack of an overall governance and coordination structure is the most pressing need in crime statistics. Currently, no entity is directly tasked with drawing inference from multiple sources of crime data, much less setting data-collection standards and common definitions. The MNCS panel noted the need for these functions in a series of conclusions (National Academies, 2018, Conclusions 3.1 and 3.2) and designated the actor that it considered best suited to establish said coordination and governance protocols (National Academies, 2018, Recommendation 3.1):

> The U.S. Office of Management and Budget (OMB) should explore the range of coordination and governance processes for the complete U.S. crime statistics enterprise—including the "new" crime categories—and then establish such a structure. The structure must ensure that all of the component functions of generating crime statistics are conducted in concordance with the sensibilities, principles, and practices of a statistical agency. It should provide for user and stakeholder involvement in the process of refining and updating the underlying classification of crime. The new governance process also needs to take responsibility for the dissemination of data products, including the production of a new form of *Crime in the United States* that includes the "new" crime categories.

The same concerns and arguments apply to cybercrime measurement as to the measurement of all crime, and we agree that coordination and governance functions are critical for producing improved cybercrime metrics. However, given how much cybercrime occurs outside the normal reach of the NIBRS and NCVS—the nation's core crime statistics sources—and given the range of public- and private-sector sources at work in the cybercrime arena, we take a slightly different approach in formalizing our guidance on overall structure. We argue for the creation of an information clearinghouse model for cybercrime data, tasking a yet-to-be-determined entity to gather and draw inference from cybercrime information obtained from multiple sources.

Conclusion 4-2: As is true of crime statistics in general, the thorough and effective measurement of cybercrime and cyber-enabled crime will remain largely unobtainable absent the development of a governance and coordination process for the collection of cybercrime reports and statistics. Cybercrime measurement is sufficiently fragmented that it is in particularly acute need of an information clearinghouse apparatus, meaning the designation of a specific party or parties to compile the various cybercrime measures that are and will be available and analyze common findings and trends.

There is a vital need for a clearinghouse and coordinating/governance structure for cybercrime statistics to canvass and analyze the full set of data sources that provide insight on cybercrime problems. This clearinghouse could perform cross-cutting data analyses that consider points of agreement and disagreement between these sources, consider their strengths and weaknesses (including any sources of bias), and build models for their use and interpretation. But, more fundamentally, there is a pressing need for a coordination and governance structure to adjudicate many of the issues raised in Chapter 1 that complicate the fit of cybercrime with existing national crime statistics. In other words, it is the panel's opinion that the structure should weigh in on counting rules for handling multivictim offenses and on the development of informative metrics beyond the basic incident count (e.g., the expanded victim count, the monetary cost of cybercrime incidents, and the level of harm inflicted). On a basic level, a coordination structure that brokers data sharing across parties may make it possible to address a long-standing, fundamental problem. If individual victims continue to find it unnatural to report cybercrime occurrences to their local law enforcement agencies (currently the only way these occurrences can enter the NIBRS), then perhaps the advice from all sides should be to advise victims to report to the IC3 (or the Federal Trade Commission, or some other entity), which could then report data to the NIBRS. But, clearly, such an arrangement would only work with effective governance of the data flows.

While the natural complement to Conclusion 4-2 would be a recommendation suggesting an organization to coordinate and govern such an information clearinghouse (or an organization to designate such a clearinghouse), we prefer to note the absence of these structures and reinforce this need without designating particular entities. We concur with the MNCS panel that the U.S. Office of Management and Budget may be ideally positioned to broker and structure the necessary discussions across federal agencies, but until the effectiveness of federal aggregations of both public- and private-sector cybercrime-related data collections at covering the range of cybercrime activity is demonstrated, we find it inadvisable to offer a concrete recommendation. Indeed, Verizon's work coordinating input from government and industry partners in its Data Breach Investigations Report (DBIR) series is a model that merits additional study. It could also be argued that the information clearinghouse function for cybercrime fits within the legally defined mission of the Bureau of Justice Statistics or the Cybersecurity & Infrastructure Security Agency, or within the stated mission of the FBI's IC3. Furthermore, the March 2022 Violence Against Women Act Reauthorization Act language on cybercrime enforcement authorized issuance of grants to a nonprofit organization to create a National Resource Center on Cybercrimes Against Individuals, among the tasks of which is to "disseminate information and statistics related to [the] incidence of cybercrimes against individuals" and conduct research on cybercrime against individuals (136 Stat. 949). Such a center might play a substantial role in data-collection efforts, but the formative grant was only issued very recently, in September 2024.[1] Finally, improvements to cybercrime measurement are resource-intensive and costly; hence, we do not deem it appropriate to make a formal recommendation that might impose a major unfunded mandate on any particular agency or organization.

An essential task of the coordination and governance structure eventually established for cybercrime measurement will be assessing data quality and using those insights to periodically revise and refine the taxonomy, categories, codes, and examples used in data collection. We view our recommended taxonomy as a first start rather than a static document. We were purposefully sparing in identifying specific cybercrime-category subdivisions, largely to accommodate the precision of data likely to be reported in the current NIBRS and NCVS systems. As collection takes place, unanticipated richness of available data might suggest the utility of new category breaks, which would ideally be considered on a periodic basis. It will also be important to review taxonomy categories, codes, and examples on a regular basis, to ensure that the materials (particularly implementation examples) are inclusive of new and emerging technologies such as artificial intelligence and quantum computing.

Businesses and Organizations as Actors in Crime and Cybercrime Data Collection

In addition to drawing insight from a variety of data resources, successful cybercrime measurement will also rely on the increased and continuing participation of businesses and organizations in reporting cybercrime incidents. This is historically difficult in the standard crime statistics context (e.g., businesses unwilling to report theft/pilferage that might suggest competitive vulnerability or weaknesses) but is even more difficult in the area of cybercrime—alongside the sheer volume of cyberattacks aimed at corporate systems and networks and the resistance to appearing vulnerable, complex

---

[1] On September 25, 2024, the grant to establish a National Resource Center on Cybercrimes Against Individuals, authorized by the Violence Against Women Act Reauthorization Act of 2022, was awarded to the nonprofit firm AEquitas; see https://www.justice.gov/opa/media/1372136/dl

issues of liability may arise for some business sectors. A financial institution that falls victim to a data breach incident may have to weigh the need to inform affected clients with perceived culpability for ineffective defense. Social media sites and internet service providers are the platforms for various interpersonal offenses and cybercrimes, and many more attempted offenses that fall short, but there is no good sense of how often they are reported to any authorities and compared with numbers of completed offenses.

To improve future cybercrime measurement, it will be important to monitor the development of CIRCIA and SEC mandatory-report systems for registering major cybersecurity incidents. Though it is not positioned as such in its formative documents, it would be ideal for the CIRCIA collection—with its broad sweep and its detailed focus on ransomware incidents—to evolve into a statistical data collection, with the resulting data illustrating sector-wide trends and informing responses and interventions to cybercrime attacks. In many ways, there are important parallels between the birth of the CIRCIA data collection (compiling data from thousands of businesses and organizations) and the dawn of the UCR Program in 1929 (drawing data from thousands of law enforcement agencies). However, a key difference between them is the mandatory-versus-voluntary nature of reporting. The histories of the UCR Program and the NIBRS provide some useful paths that the CIRCIA collection might emulate, but they also suggest development pitfalls to be avoided.

The participation of a wide variety of governmental and business actors in the compilation of the Verizon DBIR series and the work of the Information Sharing and Analysis Centers (ISACs) and Information Sharing and Analysis Organizations (ISAOs) demonstrate how information sharing can benefit collectives of businesses and organizations. The Verizon DBIR underscores the importance of data and analytics as a first step in understanding and addressing problems, and the ISACs and ISAOs incentivize information sharing by businesses and organizations that might otherwise be reluctant to do so—the reward being joint work on common problems within a particular business sector or group. Going forward, these information-sharing vehicles could evolve to include the generation of reliable, consistent statistical insights. In particular, cross-sector and multi-sector information-sharing safe havens like the National Cyber-Forensics and Training Alliance will hopefully gain a wider footing, encouraging work on solutions and defenses and alleviating frustrations that some businesses and organizations may feel about the isolation of their particular sector in a major cyberthreat landscape.

Finally, we observe that the nation's understanding of crime benefits from having a survey-based measure (i.e., the NCVS) that serves as a conceptual counterpart to police-report data on crime involving individuals. We think it is important to note that survey-based methods may have similar utility regarding business cybercrime data, though we readily note that history is not rich with success in this area. A survey of businesses' victimization experiences was part of the original National Crime Survey program, but that and other components were discontinued in the mid-1970s, prior to the redesigns that ultimately repositioned this program as the NCVS household survey. Since then, forays into commercial victimization surveys have been rare. As discussed in Chapter 2, the Bureau of Justice Statistics conducted one round of the National Computer Security Survey in 2006, asking a sample of businesses about cybersecurity and cybercrime incidents, but the survey has not been repeated. However, general improvements in conducting establishment surveys and, perhaps, increased interest in crime committed against businesses and organizations of all sizes suggest that the time may be ripe to at least revisit the concept of a commercial victimization survey, with cybercrime as an important component of any such development.

Recommendation 4-5: Pending the availability of resources to do so, the Bureau of Justice Statistics and federal agency partners should consider conducting additional rounds of the 2006 National Computer Security Survey, or otherwise field an establishment crime/cybercrime victimization survey, to collect data on crime/cybercrime victimization experiences by businesses and organizations. Such efforts should build on improvements in the conduct of establishment surveys and serve as a complementary marker of cybercrime that is not reported to authorities.

We emphasize that this is very much an aspirational recommendation, not a suggestion for immediate work. We further note that the first step in this area need not be a fully realized, national-scale, industry-comprehensive survey; structured pilot survey work involving Verizon DBIR participants or ISAC/ISAO memberships could provide useful insight on feasibility.

Exploring the Cybercrime and Cybersecurity Nexus

In closing, we return to one of our opening precepts: our panel's charge obliged us to emphasize the "crime" part of cybercrime and the fit of cybercrime within the nation's crime statistics data-collection systems. As data collection evolves, ideally incorporating the conceptual base in our recommended taxonomy, it will be important for discussions to address the "cyber" part of cybercrime as well. National crime statistics have long been criticized for not venturing much beyond incident counts—difficult though those can be to produce in their own right—but cybercrime metrics that draw from the surrounding cybersecurity realm may prove to be very valuable resources. In addition to estimates of the cost inflicted by cyber-attacks, cybersecurity monitoring data on the nature of attempted-but-failed attacks and detected-but-deflected attacks, analyzed with respect to the specific technological vectors along which the attacks are conducted, may serve to inform understanding of crime in the same manner that studies of policing, community resilience, and deterrence enhance overall understanding of crime.

References

Baum, K. (2006, April). *Identity theft, 2004* (NCJ No. 212213). Bureau of Justice Statistics. https://bjs.ojp.gov/content/pub/pdf/it04.pdf

___. (2007, November). *Identity theft, 2005* (NCJ No. 219411). Bureau of Justice Statistics. https://bjs.ojp.gov/content/pub/pdf/it05.pdf

Beals, M., DiLiema, M., & Deevy, M. (2015, July). *Framework for a taxonomy of fraud.* A joint collaboration of Financial Fraud Research Center at the Stanford Center on Longevity and the FINRA Investor Education Foundation. Stanford Center on Longevity. https://www.finrafoundation.org/sites/finrafoundation/files/2024-10/framework-taxonomy-fraud.pdf

Berris, P. G. (2023, May). *Cybercrime and the law: Primer on the Computer Fraud and Abuse Act and related statutes* (No. R47557). Congressional Research Service. https://www.congress.gov/crs-product/R47557

Biderman, A. D., & Reiss, A. J. (1967). On exploring the "dark figure" of crime. *Annals of the American Academy of Political and Social Science*, 374(1), 1–15. https://doi.org/10.1177/000271626737400102

Brenner, S. W. (2004). Cybercrime metrics: Old wine, new bottles? *Virginia Journal of Law and Technology*, 9(13), 1–52. https://www.researchgate.net/profile/Susan-Brenner/publication/265032559_Cybercrime_Metrics_Old_Wine_New_Bottles/links/5743026108ae298602ee6bd5/Cybercrime-Metrics-Old-Wine-New-Bottles.pdf

___. (2007). Cybercrime: Re-thinking crime control strategies. In Y. Jewkes (Ed.), *Crime online* (pp. 12–28). Willan Publishing. https://doi.org/10.4324/9781843925828

Brinton, J., Langton, L., Krebs, C., & Casper, M. (2023, August). *An environmental scan of cybercrime measurement: Recommendations for the National Crime Victimization Survey* (NCJ No. 306766). Prepared by RTI International for the Bureau of Justice Statistics. https://www.ojp.gov/pdffiles1/bjs/grants/306766.pdf

Bureau of Justice Statistics. (2017, December). *National Crime Victimization Survey: Technical documentation* (NCJ No. 251442). U.S. Department of Justice, Bureau of Justice Statistics. https://bjs.ojp.gov/sites/g/files/xyckuh236/files/media/document/ncvstd16.pdf

___. (2023, December). *National Incident-Based Reporting System, 2022: Extract files.* Inter-university Consortium for Political and Social Research. https://doi.org/10.3886/ICPSR38925.v1

Canadian Centre for Justice Statistics, Policing Services Program. (2008, February). *Uniform crime reporting incident-based survey.* Statistics Canada. https://www23.statcan.gc.ca/imdb-bmdi/pub/instrument/3302_Q7_V3-eng.pdf

Council of Europe. (2001). *Convention on cybercrime* (European Treaty Series No. 185). Adopted in Budapest, Hungary, on November 23, 2001. Ratified, with reservations and declarations, as Treaty Document 108-11 by the United States Senate on August 3, 2006. https://rm.coe.int/1680081561

Criminal Justice Information Services Division. (2017, February). *UCR Program Quarterly, Number 1.* Federal Bureau of Investigation. https://ucr.fbi.gov/ucr-program-quarterly/ucr-quarterly-february-2017.pdf

Davis, L. M., Golinelli, D., Beckman, R., Cotton, S. K., Anderson, R. H., Bamezai, A., Corey, C. R., Zander-Cotugno, M., Adams, J. L., Euller, R., & Steinberg, P. (2008, September). *The National Computer Security Survey (NCSS): Final methodology* (Technical Report). RAND Corporation. Prepared for the Bureau of Justice Statistics. https://www.rand.org/pubs/technical_reports/TR544.html

Federal Bureau of Investigation. (1992). *Uniform Crime Reporting handbook: National Incident-Based Reporting System edition.* U.S. Department of Justice, Bureau of Justice Statistics. https://www.ojp.gov/ncjrs/virtual-library/abstracts/uniform-crime-reporting-handbook-national-incident-based-reporting

___. (2013a, January). *A Guide to Understanding NIBRS. Uniform Crime Reporting (UCR) Program—National Incident-Based Reporting System (NIBRS) Version 1.0.* U.S. Department of Justice, Federal Bureau of Investigation. https://ucr.fbi.gov/nibrs/2013/resources/a-guide-to-understanding-nibrs

___. (2013b, June). *Criminal Justice Information Services (CJIS) Division Uniform Crime Reporting (UCR) Program—Summary Reporting System (SRS) user manual. Version 1.0.* U.S. Department of Justice, Federal Bureau of Investigation. https://dstaffordandassociates.com/wp-content/uploads/2022/02/ucr-srs-user-manual-v1.pdf

___. (2015, October). *Criminal Justice Information Services (CJIS) Division Uniform Crime Reporting (UCR) Program—National Incident-Based Reporting System (NIBRS) user manual. Version 2.0.* U.S. Department of Justice, Federal Bureau of Investigation. https://ucr.fbi.gov/nibrs/2015/resource-pages/nibrs-2015_summary_final-1.pdf

___. (2020, September). *Criminal Justice Information Services (CJIS) Division, Uniform Crime Reporting (UCR) Program—National Incident-Based Reporting System (NIBRS) user manual. Version 2019.2.1.* U.S. Department of Justice, Federal Bureau of Investigation. https://le.fbi.gov/informational-tools/ucr/ucr-technical-specifications-user-manuals-and-data-tools

___. (2021). *Internet crime report, 2020.* U.S. Department of Justice, Federal Bureau of Investigation, Internet Crime Complaint Center. https://www.ic3.gov/AnnualReport/Reports/2020_IC3Report.pdf

___. (2022). *Internet crime report, 2021.* U.S. Department of Justice, Federal Bureau of Investigation, Internet Crime Complaint Center. https://www.ic3.gov/AnnualReport/Reports/2021_IC3Report.pdf

___. (2023a, June 30). *2023.0 National Incident-Based Reporting System technical specification.* U.S. Department of Justice, Federal Bureau of Investigation, Criminal Justice Information Services Division, Uniform Crime Reporting Program. https://le.fbi.gov/file-repository/nibrs-technical-specification-063023.pdf/view

REFERENCES

___. (2023b, June 30). *2023.0 National Incident-Based Reporting System user manual.* U.S. Department of Justice, Federal Bureau of Investigation, Criminal Justice Information Services Division, Uniform Crime Reporting Program. https://le.fbi.gov/file-repository/nibrs-user-manual-063023.pdf/view

___. (2023c). *Internet crime report, 2022.* U.S. Department of Justice, Federal Bureau of Investigation, Internet Crime Complaint Center. https://www.ic3.gov/annualreport/reports/2022_ic3report.pdf

___. (2024). *Internet crime report, 2023.* U.S. Department of Justice, Federal Bureau of Investigation, Internet Crime Complaint Center. https://www.ic3.gov/annualreport/reports/2023_ic3report.pdf

Fetterhoff, M. (2024, June 5). *Trends in fraud schemes targeting older adults.* Presentation to Panel on Cybercrime Classification and Measurement. Washington, DC.

Fletcher, E. (2024, June 5). *FTC's consumer sentinel fraud categorization.* Presentation to Panel on Cybercrime Classification and Measurement. Washington, DC.

Gladden, R. M., Vivolo-Kantor, A. M., Hamburger, M. E., & Lumpkin, C. D. (2014). *Bullying surveillance among youths: Uniform definitions for public health and recommended data elements, version 1.0.* National Center for Injury Prevention and Control, Centers for Disease Control and Prevention and U.S. Department of Education. https://files.eric.ed.gov/fulltext/ED575477.pdf

Golladay, K. A. (2020). Identity theft: Nature, extent, and global response. In T. J. Holt & A. M. Bossler (Eds.), *The Palgrave handbook of international cybercrime and cyberdeviance* (pp. 981–999). Palgrave Macmillan.

Gordon, S., & Ford, R. (2006). On the definition and classification of cybercrime. *Journal in Computer Virology, 2*(1), 13–20. https://doi.org/10.1007/s11416-006-0015-z

International Association of Chiefs of Police. (1929). *Uniform crime reporting: A complete manual for police.* Report of the Committee on Uniform Crime Records. J.J. Little and Ives Company. https://widener.locate.ebsco.com/instances/6569ac44-2b12-5604-9289-e15cf69a29f5?option=author&query=James%2C%20P.%20D

Irvin, V., Wang, K., Cui, J., & Thompson, A. (2024, July). *Report on indicators of school crime and safety: 2023* (NCES 2024-145/NCJ 309126). National Center for Education Statistics. https://nces.ed.gov/pubs2024/2024145.pdf

Kaplan, F. (2016, February 21). "WarGames" and cybersecurity's debt to a Hollywood hack. *New York Times.* https://www.nytimes.com/2016/02/21/movies/wargames-and-cybersecuritys-debt-to-a-hollywood-hack.html

Langton, L., Krebs, C., Planty, M., & Berzofsky, M. (2023, August). *Assessing the quality of the National Crime Victimization Survey (NCVS) Supplemental Fraud Survey (SFS)* (Technical Report NCJ 306194). RTI International. Prepared for Bureau of Justice Statistics. https://www.ojp.gov/pdffiles1/bjs/grants/306194

Langton, L., & Planty, M. (2010, December). *Victims of identity theft, 2008* (NCJ 231680). Bureau of Justice Statistics. https://www.ojp.gov/library/publications/victims-identity-theft-2008

LaVigna, M. (2024, June). *National cyber-forensics and training alliance* [PowerPoint slides]. Presentation to Panel on Cybercrime Classification and Measurement, Washington, DC.

Marcum, C., & Higgins, G. (2019). Cybercrime. In M. Krohn, N. Handrix, G. Hall, & A. Lizotte (Eds.), *Handbooks of sociology and social research* (2nd ed.), pp. 459–475. Springer.

Morgan, R. E. (2021, April). *Financial fraud in the United States, 2017* (NCJ No. 255817). Bureau of Justice Statistics. https://bjs.ojp.gov/content/pub/pdf/ffus17.pdf

Morgan, R. E., & Truman, J. L. (2019). *Stalking victimization, 2019* (NCJ No. 301735). Bureau of Justice Statistics. https://bjs.ojp.gov/library/publications/stalking-victimization-2019

National Academies of Sciences, Engineering, and Medicine (National Academies). (2016a). *Modernizing crime statistics: Report 1: Defining and classifying crime.* The National Academies Press. https://doi.org/10.17226/23492

___. (2016b). *Preventing bullying through science, policy, and practice.* The National Academies Press. https://doi.org/10.17226/23482

___. (2018). *Modernizing crime statistics: Report 2: New systems for measuring crime.* The National Academies Press. https://doi.org/10.17226/25035

National Conference of State Legislatures. (2022, May). *Computer crime statutes.* https://www.ncsl.org/technology-and-communication/computer-crime-statutes

National Research Council. (1976). *Surveying crime.* Panel for the Evaluation of Crime Surveys. B. K. Eidson Penick (Ed.) & M. E. B. Owens III (Assoc. Ed.), Committee on National Statistics, Academy of Mathematical and Physical Sciences. The National Academy Press. https://doi.org/10.17226/19945

___. (2008). *Surveying victims: Options for conducting the National Crime Victimization Survey.* Panel to Review the Programs of the Bureau of Justice Statistics. R. M. Groves & D. L. Cork (Eds.), Committee on National Statistics and Committee on Law and Justice, Division of Behavioral and Social Sciences and Education. The National Academies Press. https://doi.org/10.17226/12090

Newman, G. R., & McNally, M. M. (2005). *Identity theft literature review* (Technical Report No. 210459). U.S. Department of Justice. Prepared for the National Institute of Justice Focus Group Meeting, January 27–28, 2005. https://www.ojp.gov/pdffiles1/nij/grants/210459.pdf

Pascale, J., Meyers, M., Martinez, M., & Fond, M. (2014). *National Crime Victimization Survey School Crime Supplement: Cognitive testing of questions on bullying.* Research Report Series (Survey Methodology No. 2014-03). https://files.eric.ed.gov/fulltext/ED584136.pdf

Phillips, K., Davidson, J. C., Farr, R. R., Burkhardt, C., Caneppele, S., & Aiken, M. P. (2022). Conceptualizing cybercrime: Definitions, typologies and taxonomies. *Forensic Sciences, 2*(2), 379–398. https://doi.org/10.3390/forensicsci2020028

Poggio, E., Kennedy, S., Chaiken, J., & Carlson, K. (1985, May). *Blueprint for the future of the Uniform Crime Reporting Program—Final report of the UCR study* (NCJ No. 098348). U.S. Department of Justice, Bureau of Justice Statistics. https://www.ojp.gov/pdffiles1/bjs/98348.pdf

Quigley, L. (2024, May). *Internet crime complaint center* [PowerPoint slides]. Presentation to Panel on Cybercrime Classification and Measurement, Washington, DC.

Rantala, R. R. (2008, September). *Cybercrime against businesses, 2005* (NCJ No. 221943). Bureau of Justice Statistics. https://static.prisonpolicy.org/scans/bjs/cb05.pdf

Sauvé, J., & Silver, W. (2024, April). *Canadian cybercrime update (UCR 2.4) from Statistics Canada* [PowerPoint slides]. Presentation to Panel on Cybercrime Classification and Measurement, Washington, DC.

Securities and Exchange Commission. (2023, August). Cybersecurity risk management, strategy, governance, and incident disclosure. *Federal Register, 88*(149), 51896–51945. https://www.federalregister.gov/d/2023-16194

Synovate. (2003). *Federal Trade Commission—Identity theft survey report.* Prepared for the Federal Trade Commission. https://www.ftc.gov/sites/default/files/documents/reports/federal-trade-commission-identity-theft-program/synovatereport.pdf

United Nations. (2024, August). *Draft United Nations convention against cybercrime: Strengthening international cooperation for combating certain crimes committed by means of information and communications technology systems and for the sharing of evidence in electronic form of serious crimes.* General Assembly Document A/AC.291/L.15, adopted by Ad Hoc Committee to Elaborate a Comprehensive International Convention on Countering the Use of Information and Communications Technologies for Criminal Purposes. https://www.unodc.org/unodc/en/cybercrime/convention/home.html

REFERENCES

United Nations Office on Drugs and Crime. (2015, March). *International Classification of Crime for Statistical Purposes (ICCS), version 1.0.* United Nations Office on Drugs and Crime. https://www.unodc.org/documents/data-and-analysis/statistics/crime/ICCS/ICCS_final-2015-March12_FINAL.pdf

U.S. Department of Homeland Security. (2023, September). *Harmonization of cyber incident reporting to the federal government.* Report to Congress prepared pursuant to Section 107(d)(1) of the Cyber Incident Reporting for Critical Infrastructure Act of 2022. https://www.dhs.gov/publication/harmonization-cyber-incident-reporting-federal-government

___. (2024, April). Cyber Incident Reporting for Critical Infrastructure Act (CIRCIA) reporting requirements. *Federal Register, 89*(66), 23644–23776. https://www.federalregister.gov/d/2024-06526

U.S. Department of Justice. (2023, January). *The report of the Attorney General pursuant to section 18(a) of Executive Order 14074: Department of Justice review of the transition of law enforcement agencies to the National Incident-Based Reporting System (NIBRS).* https://www.justice.gov/opa/speech/file/1563061/dl

U.S. Government Accountability Office. (2023, June). *Cybercrime: Reporting mechanisms vary, and agencies face challenges in developing metrics.* GAO-23-106080. U.S. Government Accountability Office. https://www.gao.gov/products/gao-23-106080

Van Buren v. United States, 593 U.S. 374, 141 S. Ct. 1648 (2021).

Verizon Business. (2024). *2024 data breach investigations report.* https://www.verizon.com/business/resources/reports/dbir/

Wall, D. (Ed.). (2001). *Crime and the internet.* Routledge.

Wall, D. (2005). The internet as a conduit for criminals. In A. Pattavina (Ed.), *Information technology and the criminal justice system* (pp. 77–98). Sage. Chapter Revised March 2010.

___. (2007). *Cybercrime—The transformation of crime in the information age.* Routledge.

Wright, S. A. (2024, April). Overview of the cyber classification compendium [PowerPoint slides]. Presentation to Panel on Cybercrime Classification and Measurement, Washington, DC.

Wright, S. A., & Parker, S. (2023). *Cyber classification compendium.* Excel spreadsheet copying cybercrime-related provisions in United States federal, United States state, and international law, prepared for and with the Canadian Association of Chiefs of Police E-Crimes Cyber Council.

Appendix A

Recent Federal Law on Cybercrime Classification

RELEVANT CYBERCRIME PROVISIONS IN VIOLENCE AGAINST WOMEN ACT REAUTHORIZATION ACT OF 2022 (P.L. 117-103; 136 STAT. 945, 950–951)

SECTION 1401. LOCAL LAW ENFORCEMENT GRANTS FOR ENFORCEMENT OF CYBERCRIMES.
   (a) DEFINITIONS.—In this section:
      (1) COMPUTER.—The term "computer" includes a computer network and an interactive electronic device.
      (2) CYBERCRIME AGAINST INDIVIDUALS.—The term "cybercrime against individuals"—
         (A) means a criminal offense applicable in the area under the jurisdiction of the relevant State, Indian Tribe, or unit of local government that involves the use of a computer to harass, threaten, stalk, extort, coerce, cause fear to, or intimidate an individual, or without consent distribute intimate images of an adult, except that use of a computer need not be an element of such an offense; and
         (B) does not include the use of a computer to cause harm to a commercial entity, government agency, or non-natural person.

SECTION 1403. NATIONAL STRATEGY, CLASSIFICATION, AND REPORTING ON CYBERCRIME.
   (a) DEFINITIONS.—In this section:

(1) COMPUTER.—The term "computer" includes a computer network and any interactive electronic device.
(2) CYBERCRIME AGAINST INDIVIDUALS.—The term "cybercrime against individuals" has the meaning given the term in section 1401.

(b) NATIONAL STRATEGY.—The Attorney General shall develop a national strategy to—
(1) reduce the incidence of cybercrimes against individuals;
(2) coordinate investigations of cybercrimes against individuals by Federal law enforcement agencies;
(3) increase the number of Federal prosecutions of cybercrimes against individuals; and
(4) develop an evaluation process that measures rates of cybercrime victimization and prosecutorial rates among Tribal and culturally specific communities.

(c) CLASSIFICATION OF CYBERCRIMES AGAINST INDIVIDUALS FOR PURPOSES OF CRIME REPORTS.—In accordance with the authority of the Attorney General under section 534 of title 28, United States Code, the Director of the Federal Bureau of Investigation shall—
(1) design and create within the Uniform Crime Reports a category for offenses that constitute cybercrimes against individuals;
(2) to the extent feasible, within the category established under paragraph (1), establish subcategories for each type of cybercrime against individuals that is an offense under Federal or State law;
(3) classify the category established under paragraph (1) as a Part I crime in the Uniform Crime Reports; and
(4) classify each type of cybercrime against individuals that is an offense under Federal or State law as a Group A offense for the purpose of the National Incident-Based Reporting System.

(d) ANNUAL SUMMARY.—The Attorney General shall publish an annual summary of the information reported in the Uniform Crime Reports and the National Incident-Based Reporting System relating to cybercrimes against individuals, including an evaluation of the implementation process for the national strategy developed under subsection (b) and outcome measurements on its impact on Tribal and culturally specific communities.

APPENDIX A

BETTER CYBERCRIME METRICS ACT (P.L. 117-116)
SECTION 1. SHORT TITLE.
This Act may be cited as the "Better Cybercrime Metrics Act".

SEC. 2. FINDINGS.
Congress finds the following:
(1) Public polling indicates that cybercrime could be the most common crime in the United States.
(2) The United States lacks comprehensive cybercrime data and monitoring, leaving the country less prepared to combat cybercrime that threatens national and economic security.
(3) In addition to existing cybercrime vulnerabilities, the people of the United States and the United States have faced a heightened risk of cybercrime during the COVID-19 pandemic.
(4) Subsection (c) of the Uniform Federal Crime Reporting Act of 1988 (34 U.S.C. 41303(c)) requires the Attorney General to "acquire, collect, classify, and preserve national data on Federal criminal offenses as part of the Uniform Crime Reports" and requires all Federal departments and agencies that investigate criminal activity to "report details about crime within their respective jurisdiction to the Attorney General in a uniform matter and on a form prescribed by the Attorney General".

SEC. 3. CYBERCRIME TAXONOMY.
(a) In General.—Not later than 90 days after the date of enactment of this Act, the Attorney General shall seek to enter into an agreement with the National Academy of Sciences to develop a taxonomy for the purpose of categorizing different types of cybercrime and cyber-enabled crime faced by individuals and businesses.
(b) Development.—In developing the taxonomy under subsection (a), the National Academy of Sciences shall—
  (1) ensure the taxonomy is useful for the Federal Bureau of Investigation to classify cybercrime in the National Incident-Based Reporting System, or any successor system;
  (2) consult relevant stakeholders, including—
    (A) the Cybersecurity and Infrastructure Security Agency of the Department of Homeland Security;
    (B) Federal, State, and local law enforcement agencies;
    (C) criminologists and academics;
    (D) cybercrime experts;
    (E) business leaders; and

(3) take into consideration relevant taxonomies developed by non-governmental organizations, international organizations, academies, or other entities.
(c) Report.—Not later than 1 year after the date on which the Attorney General enters into an agreement under subsection (a), the National Academy of Sciences shall submit to the appropriate committees of Congress a report detailing and summarizing—
  (1) the taxonomy developed under subsection (a); and
  (2) any findings from the process of developing the taxonomy under subsection (a).
(d) Authorization of Appropriations.—There are authorized to be appropriated to carry out this section $1,000,000.

SEC. 4. CYBERCRIME REPORTING.

(a) In General.—Not later than 2 years after the date of enactment of this Act, the Attorney General shall establish a category in the National Incident-Based Reporting System, or any successor system, for the collection of cybercrime and cyber-enabled crime reports from Federal, State, and local officials.
(b) Recommendations.—In establishing the category required under subsection (a), the Attorney General shall, as appropriate, incorporate recommendations from the taxonomy developed under section 3(a).

SEC. 5. NATIONAL CRIME VICTIMIZATION SURVEY.

(a) In General.—Not later than 540 days after the date of enactment of this Act, the Director of the Bureau of Justice Statistics, in coordination with the Director of the Bureau of the Census, shall include questions relating to cybercrime victimization in the National Crime Victimization Survey.
(b) Authorization of Appropriations.—There are authorized to be appropriated to carry out this section $2,000,000.

SEC. 6. GAO STUDY ON CYBERCRIME METRICS.

Not later than 180 days after the date of enactment of this Act, the Comptroller General of the United States shall submit to Congress a report that assesses—
  (1) the effectiveness of reporting mechanisms for cybercrime and cyber-enabled crime in the United States; and
  (2) disparities in reporting data between—
    (A) data relating to cybercrime and cyber-enabled crime; and
    (B) other types of crime data.

Legislative History: S. 2629 introduced in the Senate August 5, 2021; reported by Judiciary Committee December 1, 2021; passed Senate without amendment by unanimous consent December 7, 2021. Received in the House and held at the desk December 8, 2021. Considered under suspension of the rules on March 28, 2022, and passed by the House 377–48 on March 29, 2022. Signed into law as Public Law No. 117-116 on May 5, 2022.

Appendix B

Detailed Definitions and Inclusions, Panel's Recommended Classification of Cybercrime

Code	Offense, Definition, and Inclusions/Exclusions
1	**ACTS TARGETED AGAINST MACHINES, DATA, OR SYSTEMS** Unlawful acts that are cyberdependent, in that computers, data, or systems are the target of the action and the offense could not happen without a computer or system
1A	Ransomware Deployment of malware[1] to render files on the computer/system inaccessible until a ransom[2] is paid • *Note:* Selection of this category should require that an offense of extortion/blackmail be coded for the incident

---

[1] *Malware* is software developed for any malicious purpose, regardless of the type of harm to be created by the software (i.e., system monitoring or keystroke logging) or the manner by which it is deployed (e.g., direct insertion onto computer, email attachment, or link distributed via social media). Malware also includes alternative development processes such as Malware-as-a-Service in which the malware developer leases or sells the code to other actors to deploy after customization. Malware may take the form of or be described using terms including virus, worm, trojan, spyware, scareware, rootkit, exploit kit, or bots/botnets.

[2] *Ransom* is the payment demanded in return for the release of something that has been held hostage. In the context of ransomware, the ransom is commonly a payment in untraceable cryptocurrency, though it need not be a monetary payment; it may be performance of a particular action.

- *Include:*
  - Any like offense in which ransom is demanded to restore access, whether the malware works through encrypting files or through locking users out/altering their permissions
  - Any like offense in which ransom is demanded to prevent removal of data or public release of sensitive information
  - Involvement in the production of Ransomware-as-a-Service
- *Exclude:* Any like offense in which ransom is not demanded

1B	Unlawful Access or Deprivation of Access Malicious cyberactivity intended to obtain access to computers, data, or systems—without permission or in excess of authorized use—or to make a computer or system unavailable to other users • *Include:* — Cybertrespassing — Unlawful access to a computer, network, or system (or the unsuccessful attempt to gain such access) to compromise a system or disrupt a service, including exploitation of vulnerability,[3] unauthorized login attempts,[4] spoofing or manipulating Domain Name System (DNS) servers to obtain access, and general attempts to bypass or override a network's access control system—as well as login via a compromised account using stolen (legitimate) access credentials — Denial-of-Service or Distributed Denial-of-Service attacks intended to disrupt the normal processing and response capacity of targeted systems by, for example, mass bombardment of requests, queries, network packets, or emails directed toward a service or network[5] — Sabotage of system access, or deliberate physical or logical activities that make the targeted system inaccessible to other users (rather than damage, change, or delete the system content)

---

[3]*Exploitation of vulnerability attempts* can take such forms as SQL Injection, malicious SQL language to interfere with database queries; Cross-Site Scripting, malicious scripts introduced into web pages and applications; and file-inclusion techniques, using loopholes in web applications to input and execute local or remote malicious files.

[4]*Unauthorized login attempts* include attempts to gain access to a system via routine access control mechanisms, such as brute forcing (i.e., sequentially stepping through possible credentials/passkeys), password cracking (i.e., breaking the protective cryptographic keys to login credentials), dictionary attack (i.e., attempting login using credentials previously archived in a dictionary), or password spraying (i.e., attempting login via commonly used and repeated passwords across multiple user names/accounts).

[5]Such attacks may be known as email bombs, floods, amplification attacks, or reflection attacks; attacks specific to telephone communications may be termed Telephony Denial of Service.

APPENDIX B 115

	1C	Unlawful Interference, Tampering, or Content Release Malicious cyberactivity intended to alter, change, distort, or undermine the integrity of the information content or the functioning of a network or system, or to exfiltrate/release data without authorization • *Include:* — Unlawful access to a computer, network, or system to alter or destroy information or the functioning of a network or system, including Man-in-the-Middle attacks[6] — Unlawful data breach or data exfiltration, in which information is accessed and sold, leaked, or otherwise disseminated without authorization
	1D	Other Acts Targeted Against Machines, Data, or Systems Other malicious cyberactivity for purposes not previously listed • *Include:* — Other acts of creating, developing, or distributing malware for purposes not previously listed, such as Command and Control (C2, C&C)[7] — Unlawful active or passive information gathering[8] on systems or networks that is not intended to alter information content or change system functioning — Advanced Persistent Threats, or programs of sustained, layered cyberattacks (potentially involving multiple attack modes), premised on stealth and long-term presence and monitoring on a system or network to achieve criminal goals — As applied to computers, data, or systems critical to states and nations, such cyber-dependent acts could be termed political interference, cyberwarfare, or espionage
2		**FRAUD AND ACTS TARGETED AGAINST PROPERTY** Unlawful cyberactivity premised on the use of deceit or other dishonest conduct to result in the loss of property (including data and money) by an individual or organization

---

[6]*Man-in-the-Middle* attacks are malicious acts against communication channels for purposes of intercepting and potentially modifying transmitted data, without the knowledge of the communicating parties. Such acts specifically targeting mobile devices (e.g., distribution of fake apps) have been termed *Man-in-the-Mobile* attacks.

[7]*Command and Control* (C2, C&C) is use of a bot or botnet to seize control of a computer or system to execute commands on another system or to channel information between systems.

[8]In this context, *information gathering* includes such acts as scanning (i.e., scanning a network to identify open ports or services or active subsystems), sniffing (i.e., logical or physical interception and reading of network traffic or communications), or transfer of DNS zones.

	2A	Identity Theft Unlawful cyberactivity resulting in the possession or acquisition of personal or financial identifying information without the consent of the affected person or the use of said identifying information to further any unlawful purpose • *Note:* Selection of this category should require that an offense of identity theft be coded for the incident • *Include:* — Consumer financial and product/services fraud perpetrated through cyberactivity against individual persons that involves the use of personal or financial identifying information to misuse an existing account (e.g., bank, credit card, other financial service, email/social media) in a person's name, to open a new account in a person's name, or for other unlawful purposes — Unlawful impersonation of another person
	2B	Fraud Unlawful cyberactivity premised on the use of deceit, deception, persuasion, or other dishonest conduct to obtain some benefit or consequence or to evade a liability, wherein said benefit or consequence may be nonexistent, unnecessary, never intended to be provided, or deliberately distorted • *Note:* Selection of this category should require that an offense of fraud be coded for the incident • *Include:* — Information-gathering actions based on use of fraud and deception, including phishing[9] and social engineering, or that enable phishing or information gathering (e.g., hosting or constructing a website that looks like a trusted authority as a front for phishing; pharming[10])

---

[9]*Phishing* involves attempted elicitation of sensitive information from individuals by deceptively pretending to be a legitimate, trustworthy entity. Specific labels are commonly applied to phishing based on the medium by which the deceptive communications are delivered—*whaling* when messages are delivered by email, *smishing/SMS phishing* when delivered by short message service (SMS) text messages, or *vishing/voice phishing* when done by telephone or Voice over Internet Protocol. When phishing is done against specifically targeted recipients (i.e., employees of a particular company) rather than a broader, "public" net casting, the practice has been termed *spear phishing*.

[10]*Pharming* is the redirection of users from a legitimate/trusted website to a fraudulent, attacker-controlled website, based on the manipulation of DNS servers or stored caches, such that the redirection is unknown to the user.

		— Consumer financial and product/services fraud perpetrated through cyberactivity against individual persons but not directly premised upon acquiring and using personal or financial identifying information, including false pretenses/swindle/confidence game[11]
		— Wire fraud, or the use of computer or electronic communications in the commission or furtherance of a fraud against a person or an organization, including variants such as advanced fee/overpayment, Business Email Compromise/Email Account Compromise, confidence/romance schemes
		— Fraud against businesses, establishments, nonprofit organizations, or government agencies perpetrated through cyberactivity, including false representation, misrepresentation, impersonation of a business or institution,[12] and welfare fraud
		— Pump-and-dump schemes[13] and similar forms of securities and investment fraud in which the promulgation of misleading information by electronic means is central to the offense
		— Tech support fraud against persons or organizations, in which the offender impersonates technical support or customer service personnel for fraudulent purposes
	2C	Other Acts Targeted Against Property Other fraudulent or property-affecting cyberactivity not previously described • *Include:*
		— Computer-related forgery or counterfeiting
		— Computer-related intellectual property offenses, including copyright infringements, trademark-related offenses, and digital piracy
		— Cryptolaundering (money laundering in cryptocurrency)
3		**ACTS AGAINST INDIVIDUALS, NONSEXUAL IN NATURE** Unlawful cyberactivity, not purely of a sexual nature, that is meant to instill fear or emotional distress in another person

---

[11] *False pretenses/swindle/confidence game* offenses include such variants as investment fraud (e.g., monetary and real estate), lottery/sweepstakes/inheritance, and nonpayment/nondelivery.

[12] *False representation* is the unauthorized use of the name of an institution for purposes of carrying out fraudulent activities. *Government impersonation* is the impersonation of a government official or office to perpetrate fraud.

[13] In the "pump" phase of a *pump-and-dump scheme*, perpetrators artificially inflate the price of a stock they have acquired at low cost through use of fraudulent and deceptive communications (primarily through electronic means) to make the low-cost stock attractive to buyers. The stock is then sold during the "dump" phase—the massive sale typically causing the stock price to plummet and causing loss to investors. See https://www.investor.gov/introduction-investing/investing- basics/glossary/pump-and-dump-schemes

- *Include:*
  - Cyberharassment (harassment by cyberactivity, including social media)[14]
  - Cyberbullying (bullying by cyberactivity)[15]
  - Cyberstalking (stalking by cyberactivity)[16]
  - Unlawful trolling, or the deliberate posting of inflammatory or derogatory comments on social media or electronic forums for the purpose of eliciting strong reactions from others, constituting more than benign chatter but falling short of the course-of-conduct nature of harassment, bullying, or stalking
  - Doxing (or doxxing), or the online posting of another individual's personal identifying information to threaten, harass, intimidate, or humiliate an individual or incite a violent crime against that individual[17]

---

[14] As in National Academies of Sciences, Engineering, and Medicine (2016a; National Academies), *harassment* is defined as engaging in an unlawful course of conduct of words or actions that, being directed at a specific person, annoys, alarms, or causes substantial emotional distress in that person. In turn, a *course of conduct* is a pattern composed of a series of two or more acts over a period of time, however short, demonstrating a continuity of purpose.

[15] As in National Academies (2016a), *bullying* is a variant of criminal harassment in which the offender exploits a real or perceived imbalance of power (either physical or social) with the objective of dominating and belittling victim(s); *cyberbullying* is the use of social media and electronic communications to conduct those behaviors. As in National Academies (2016a, p. 219), we note that state law commonly addresses the offense of bullying in education code rather than penal/criminal code, treating bullying as behavior between minors that is handled by local schools; however, states have taken a firmer hand in criminalizing cyberbullying in penal code language, likely because of incidences of adults impersonating children to conduct bullying behavior and communications.

[16] As in National Academies (2016a), *stalking* is the act of engaging in a course of conduct directed at a specific person—including but not limited to acts in which the perpetrator follows, monitors, observes, surveils, or threatens the victim—in which the perpetrator knows or should know that the course of conduct would cause a reasonable person to fear for his or her safety or the safety of a third person (e.g., a family member), or to suffer other emotional distress. *Cyberstalking* is the use of social media and electronic communications to conduct those behaviors.

[17] *Doxing* could also be classified under category 2A as identity theft, given the nature of the information being unlawfully disclosed. However, we classify it here following the lead of U.S. federal law, which includes "knowingly mak[ing] restricted personal information about a covered person [or member of their immediate family] publicly available [with] the intent to threaten, intimidate, or incite the commission of a crime of violence" against the person (18 U.S.C. § 119) under the broad heading of assault. The provision defines "covered person" as any officer or employee of the federal government acting in their official duties; any juror, witness, informant, or officer of any court of the United States; or any state/local law enforcement officer being doxed in retaliation for their participation in a federal criminal investigation.

APPENDIX B

	— Swatting, or the reporting of a false violent crime emergency to prompt a large response by law enforcement personnel as a means of threat or harassment, when there is a cyber hook to the offense (e.g., use of Caller ID spoofing, phishing, or other techniques)
	— Computer-related acts of extortion or coercion against an individual, not consistent with ransomware but also not purely of a sexual or prurient nature
4	**ACTS AGAINST INDIVIDUALS, SEXUAL IN NATURE** Unlawful cyberactivity of a sexual or prurient nature that is meant to instill fear or emotional distress in another person • *Include:* — Unlawful possession, creation, access to, or distribution of child sexual exploitation material or child pornography through electronic means — Unlawful possession, creation, access to, or distribution of adult sexual exploitation material through electronic means — Unlawful cyberactivity for purposes of grooming or enticement of prospective victims of sexual exploitation — Unlawful online sexual extortion (sextortion) of children or adults, typically in which payment is demanded to prevent the release or publication of intimate images — Other unlawful image-based sexual abuse, including cyberflashing (unsolicited sending of intimate or prurient images), "revenge porn," and nonconsensual pornography
5	**ACTS TARGETED AGAINST GROUPS** Malicious cyberactivity involving the dissemination of abusive or unsolicited content to groups of individuals • *Include:* — Email bombs or excessive spam, involving the unlawful sending of an unusually large quantity of unsolicited or unwanted email messages — Unlawful computer-related actions against groups based on protected characteristics, including unlawful hate speech and religious offenses — Computer-related acts of terrorism and radicalization — Unlawful computer-related incitement to violence
6	**ACTS INVOLVING INCIDENTAL TECHNOLOGY USE** Criminal acts that may involve the use of computers or networks but in which the cyberactivity is not central to the execution of the crime • *Include:* — Criminal communications — Electronic records of unlawful gaming and gambling

	— Using information and communication technology to lure a victim into a physical attack
	— Computer and telecommunications use in money laundering, including money muling
NA	ACTS WITH NO CYBER/COMPUTER INVOLVEMENT

SOURCES: Generated by the panel, drawing in particular from Phillips et al. (2022), National Academies (2016a), and Wright and Parker (2023).

Appendix C

Cybercrime Offenses Defined in Current Systems and Law

CYBERCRIME OFFENSES DEFINED IN FEDERAL AND STATE LAW

Federal Law

"Cybercrime" was not formally defined in federal law until the cybercrime provisions in the Violence Against Women Act Reauthorization Act of 2022, which set forth a two-pronged definition. In that act, "cybercrime against individuals" is defined as "a criminal offense [. . .] that involves the use of a computer to harass, threaten, stalk, extort, coerce, cause fear to, or intimidate an individual." The definition also includes nonconsensual pornography, commonly known as revenge porn, which is an offense to "without consent distribute intimate images of an adult, except that use of a computer need not be an element of such an offense" (136 Stat. 945).

Of course, cybercrime-related concepts were defined in federal law prior to 2022, just under different terminology. Wire fraud was likely the earliest instance of a crime being defined by the technical means of communications technology used in its perpetration. Several other computer-based crimes were added by the Computer Fraud and Abuse Act (CFAA) in 1984 and 1986, initially and famously sparked by reactions to the 1983 film *WarGames* (Berris, 2023; Kaplan, 2016).

A concise summary of key cybercrime offenses defined under federal law follows:

- *Wire fraud (18 U.S.C. § 1343):* "Fraud by wire, radio, or television" was originally defined in statute in 1952 (66 Stat. 722) as "having devised or intending to devise any scheme or artifice to defraud, or for obtaining money or property by means of false or fraudulent pretenses, representations, or promises, transmits or causes to be transmitted by means of interstate wire, radio, or television communication, any writings, signs, signals, pictures, or sounds for the purpose of executing such scheme or artifice." This was amended in 1956 to read "transmitted by means of wire, radio, or television communication in interstate or foreign commerce" (70 Stat. 523).

- *Fraud and related activity in connection with computers (CFAA; 18 U.S.C. § 1030):* The first three offenses under this heading were included in the original CFAA language in 1984 (P.L. 98-473; 98 Stat. 2190), with the others added during substantial revision in 1986 (100 Stat. 1213) and later amendments.
  — *Cyberespionage*, or unauthorized access via computer to national security information: Amended in 1996 to include sharing (i.e., communicating, delivering, or transmitting) or unauthorized retention of such information
  — *Unauthorized access to and obtaining of certain information via computer:* The original 1984 language references "information contained in a financial record of a financial institution [or] contained in a file of a consumer reporting agency on a consumer"; subsequent amendments added "information from any department or agency of the United States" and "information from any protected computer"
  — *Government computer trespassing,* or unauthorized access to U.S. federal government computer resources: The original 1984 language included "knowingly uses, modifies, destroys, or discloses information" in federal government computers as an element of the offense, but this detail was subsequently removed
  — *Computer fraud,* or unauthorized access to a computer with the intent to commit fraud, resulting in the obtaining of anything of value, "unless the object of the fraud and the thing obtained consists only of the use of the computer and the value of such use is not more than $5,000 in any 1-year period"
  — *Computer damage, including the introduction of malware:* Specifically, the legal text refers to the "transmission of a program, information, code, or command" that causes damage; offense also includes reckless or unintentional damage to computers done through intentional unauthorized access short of the introduction of malicious code
  — *Trafficking in passwords or other mechanisms for unauthorized access* to U.S. federal government computers, with the

restriction that "such trafficking affects interstate or foreign commerce"
  — *Extortionate threats to damage computers or disclose information obtained through unauthorized access*, provided that the threats are made in the line of "interstate or foreign commerce" (e.g., via the internet). Among the types of threats covered by the section are a "demand or request for money or [an]other thing of value in relation to damage to a protected computer, where such damage was caused to facilitate the extortion"; interpreting the placement of encryption locks on computer files as "damage," this clause has been used to prosecute federal ransomware cases (Berris, 2023, pp. 24–25)

Attempt to commit these offenses and conspiracy to commit these offenses are both considered offenses under the CFAA. Generally, the act applies to offenses involving "protected computers," defined as computers used by the U.S. federal government or financial institutions, used in part of a voting system for federal elections, or used in interstate or foreign commerce—the latter clause of which has commonly been interpreted by the courts as including "any computer connected to the internet" (Berris, 2023, p. 6).

- *Cyberstalking (18 U.S.C. § 2261A(2))*: "[U]ses the mail, any interactive computer service or electronic communication service or electronic communication system of interstate commerce, or any other facility of interstate or foreign commerce to engage in a course of conduct that [places] that person in reasonable fear of the death of or serious bodily injury to [that person or an immediate family member, spouse/intimate partner, or pet/service animal/emotional support animal/horse of that person]," or that "causes, attempts to cause, or would be reasonably expected to cause substantial emotional distress" to any of those parties. This course of conduct is done "with the intent to kill, injure, harass, intimidate, or place under surveillance with intent to kill, injure, harass, or intimidate another person." Original interstate stalking language of § 2261A became law in 1996; the cyberstalking provisions were introduced in 2006 (119 Stat. 2987; part of Violence Against Women and Department of Justice Reauthorization Act of 2005) and amended in 2013 (127 Stat. 78; part of the Violence Against Women Act Reauthorization Act of 2013).
- *Identity theft (18 U.S.C. § 1028(a)(7))*: "[K]nowingly transfers, possesses, or uses, without lawful authority, a means of identification of another person with the intent to commit, or to aid or abet, or in connection with, any unlawful activity that constitutes a violation of Federal law, or that constitutes a felony under any

applicable State or local law." Section 1028(c) includes "the transfer of a document by electronic means" as a triggering circumstance. This language was added by the Identity Theft and Assumption Deterrence Act of 1998 (P.L. 105-318; 112 Stat. 3007). In 2004, the Identity Theft Penalty Enhancement Act (P.L. 108-275, 118 Stat. 831) defined "aggravated identity theft" as "knowingly transfers, possesses, or uses, without lawful authority, a means of identification of another person [...] during and in relation to" a specified set of federal felony violations (e.g., false statements in acquiring a firearm and identity theft in connection with nationality and citizenship).

In addition, some specific categories of offenses defined in federal law may be said to include a cyber or computer component to them. For instance, the chapter of federal statute defining fraud and related offenses includes several variants that have a distinct cyber component to them, including 18 U.S.C. § 1029 and § 1037 concerning access device fraud (i.e., automated teller machine cards) and multiple deceptive email messages, respectively.

As noted in Chapter 1, it is beyond the panel's scope to discuss the adequacy or coverage of federal or state cybercrime law. But it is relevant and worth observing that key words in definitions are periodically the focus of legal challenges. For instance, it remains to be seen whether or how Congress will react to a recent challenge to the federal CFAA's underlying "(un)authorized access" definition. In *Van Buren v. United States* (2021), the U.S. Supreme Court reversed the conviction of a police officer under the terms of the CFAA. The officer, who had credentialed access to license plate databases, ran a search on a particular license plate in return for money. A divided Supreme Court ruled that the strict letter of the CFAA—defining "exceeds authorized access" to mean "to access a computer with authorization and to use such access to obtain or alter information in the computer that the accesser is not entitled so to obtain or alter" (18 U.S.C. § 1030(e)(6))—does not cover purpose-based violations, the misuse of information to which a database user is otherwise permitted to access. That is, the officer may have violated departmental policy in running a search on a law enforcement database for non-law-enforcement purposes but not the federal CFAA—a result that may be consequential in other data-related suits.

State Law

Though exact nomenclature and detail varies greatly across the states, a 2022 canvass by the National Conference of State Legislatures (2022) found that all 50 states have some form of computer crime statute in their penal or criminal codes—Colorado seemingly being unique among the states in explicitly labeling the base offense as "cybercrime" (having switched from "computer crime" in 2018; C.R.S.A. § 18-5.5-102 [West]). The core computer crime typically involves one or more basic elements from the federal CFAA, criminalizing unauthorized access and computer trespass as well as more direct hacking/computer tampering (see also Brinton et al., 2023). The National Conference of State Legislatures, (2022) summary observed that at least 26 states explicitly reference denial-of-service attacks in their statutes, 12 states explicitly reference ransomware/computer extortion, and 23 states explicitly address phishing or social engineering.

EVOLUTION OF THE HANDLING OF CYBERCRIME AND COMPUTER CRIME IN REVISIONS OF NATIONAL INCIDENT-BASED REPORTING SYSTEM MANUALS

Original "NIBRS Edition" Uniform Crime Reporting Manual, 1992

- *"Offender(s) Suspected of Using Computer Equipment"* as part of original data specification: The data element for Offender(s) Suspected of Using has been part of the National Incident-Based Reporting System (NIBRS) since the system's inception. In the original handbook, it is described as "indicat[ing] whether any of the offenders in the incident were suspected of consuming alcohol or using drugs/narcotics during or shortly before the incident; or of using a computer, computer terminal, or other computer equipment to perpetrate the crime." Any or all of the categories—A (Alcohol), C (Computer Equipment), or D (Drugs/Narcotics)—could be coded for the incident. Moreover, the use of computer equipment played into one example illustrating the data element's use: "Example (4): A computer 'hacker' used his personal computer and a telephone modem to gain access to the company's computer and steal proprietary data. 'Computer Equipment' should be reported" (Federal Bureau of Investigation, 1992, p. 38).
- *Guidance to code computer crime offenses using other defined offenses*: In the handbook's Offense Lookup Table, the guidance for "Computer Crime" is to "classify same as substantive offense, e.g., Larceny-Theft; Embezzlement." There is no mention of ticking the Offender(s) Suspected of Using data element in those offenses (Federal Bureau of Investigation, 1992, p. 77).
- *Used to illustrate series/continuing activity nature of some offenses*: One example raised relative to deciding how many incidents to count reads as follows: "Over a period of 18 months, a computer programmer working for a bank manipulated the

bank's computer and systematically embezzled $70,000. The continuing criminal activity constituted a single 'incident' involving the crime of embezzlement" (Federal Bureau of Investigation, 1992, p. 28).

NIBRS User Manual Version 1.0, 2013

- *"Capturing Computer Crime" advanced as major benefit of NIBRS participation:* Appendix material arguing for the benefits to local law enforcement of fully participating in the NIBRS included the following entry: "To combat the growing problem of computer crime (i.e., crimes directed at and perpetrated through the use of computers and related equipment), the NIBRS provides the capability to indicate whether a computer was the object of the reported crime and to indicate whether the offenders used computer equipment to perpetrate a crime" (Federal Bureau of Investigation, 2013a, p. 141).
- *Offender Suspected of Using data element retained:* Now numbered as Data Element 8, the Offender Suspected of Using item in the 2013 manual contained an identical short definition and response codes as in 1992, save for the addition of an N (Not Applicable) category (Federal Bureau of Investigation, 2013a, p. 71). However, the 2013 version provided no examples for the use of Data Element 8.
- *Continued guidance to code computer crime offenses using other defined offenses:* In the manual's Offense Lookup Table, the guidance for "Computer Crime" is to "classify same as substantive offense, e.g., Larceny-Theft, Embezzlement, or Fraud Offenses." Accordingly, the table notes that the proper offense code "depends on circumstances" and could deem the computer crime either a Group A or Group B offense (Federal Bureau of Investigation, 2013a, p. 47).
- *Definition of Wire Fraud expanded to include computer fraud:* The 2013 iteration of the handbook retained the base definition of Wire Fraud from 1992—"the use of an electric or electronic communications facility to intentionally transmit a false and/or deceptive message in furtherance of a fraudulent activity." It limited the applicability of Wire Fraud to those cases in which "telephone, teletype, micro-relay facilities, etc., are used in the commission or furtherance of a fraud" (Federal Bureau of Investigation, 1992, p. 16). However, the 2013 manual expanded Wire Fraud to include a broader array of communication technologies—cases where "telephone, teletype, computers, e-mail, text messages, etc., are used in the commission or furtherance of a fraud." "For example, if someone uses a computer to order products through a

fraudulent online auction site and pays for the products but never receives them, LEAs [law enforcement agencies] should classify the incident as" Wire Fraud (Federal Bureau of Investigation, 2013a, p. 28).
- *Identity Documents and Identity–Intangible among many new Property Type codes:* Identity–Intangible was a first foray into intangible data or information being a property type subject to theft or damage by criminal offenses logged in the NIBRS (Federal Bureau of Investigation, 2013a, p. 96).
- *Used to illustrate "same time and place" nature of some offenses:* The 2013 manual repeated the 1992 handbook's example of systematic embezzlement by computer constituting a single incident, save for insertion of the clarifying note that the continuing criminal activity was *"against the same victim"* (emphasis original) and so constituted a single incident (Federal Bureau of Investigation, 2013a, p. 11).

Version 2.0, 2015

- *Addition of Identity Theft and Hacking/Computer Invasion offenses, following their approval by the director of the Federal Bureau of Investigation in April 2014:* Identity Theft, defined as "wrongfully obtaining and using another person's personal data (e.g., name, date of birth, Social Security number, driver's license number, credit card number)," and Hacking/Computer Invasion, defined as "wrongfully gaining access to another person's or institution's computer software, hardware, or networks without authorized permissions or security clearances," were added as new categories of Fraud Offenses, broadly classified as Offenses Against Property (Federal Bureau of Investigation, 2015, p. 31). Wire Fraud was defined and explained identically to the 2013 manual, preserving the computer-related content.
- *Addition of Cyberspace as Location of offense, following the approval of the director of the Federal Bureau of Investigation in fall 2014:* Location category 58, Cyberspace, was defined as "a virtual or internet-based network of two or more computers in separate locations which communicate either through wireless or wire connections" (Federal Bureau of Investigation, 2015, p. 84). Four examples underscore the apparent internet focus of the location code rather than general computer involvement (Federal Bureau of Investigation, 2015, pp. 84–85):
"Police received a phone call from an individual who reported he recently received a letter from a local business informing him that

the business' computers were recently hacked from an external source and the customer's personal information might have been compromised. The individual then reported he noticed someone had opened credit cards and other loans in his name." In this scenario, the offense would be coded as Identity Theft and the location as Cyberspace because "this crime could not have been committed" in this manner "had the internet not been available."

"Police received a phone call from an individual who reported he recently received a letter from the Target Corporation, informing him that the business' computers were recently stolen and the customer's personal information may have been compromised. The individual then reported he noticed someone had opened credit cards and other loans in his name." In this scenario, the offense would still be Identity Theft, but the location would be entered as Department/Discount Store "since this incident is not cyberspace related. The fact the internet exists has nothing to do with the commission of this crime."

"Police received a phone call from a business that reported their computers were recently hacked based on information identified by their Information Technology staff. The business reported the hacking/invasion offense appeared to have come from an internet address located in Iran." Hacking/Computer Invasion would be the offense and Cyberspace the location "because if cyberspace had not been available, this crime could not have been committed."

"Police received a phone call from a business that stated an employee had used his computer to download and steal trade secret information from the company. The company stated the individual did not have access to the information and fraudulently accessed the folders where the information was located." Hacking/Computer Invasion would be the offense, but Commercial/Office Building would be the location type because, "even though a computer was used to steal the information, the subject used an internal system and could have directly accessed the information without utilizing the internet."

- *Data Element 8, Offender Suspected of Using, defined and described identically as in Version 1.0,* including the omission of any examples (Federal Bureau of Investigation, 2015, p. 76).

Version 2019.2, 2020, and Subsequent Revisions

- *Revision of Data Element 8 (Offender Suspected of Using) to focus on handheld devices:* The February 2017 Uniform Crime Reporting Program Quarterly bulletin announced a new policy to collect information on vehicular/vessel negligent manslaughter and negligent assault offenses—that is, deaths and injuries caused by under-the-influence or distracted drivers—which would require the "modification of Data Element 8 (Offender Suspected of Using) to include 'handheld devices' with Computer Equipment" (Criminal Justice Information Services Division, 2017). The revision logs in versions of the NIBRS User Manual beginning in 2020 suggest that the change completed the approval process and went into effect on January 1, 2019 (Federal Bureau of Investigation, 2020, p. ii). In the manual, the name and general definition of Data Element 8 are kept the same ("suspected of [...] using computer equipment to perpetrate the crime"), but the valid data value is revised to "C = Computer Equipment (Handheld Devices)"—suggesting not just the inclusion of cell/smartphones as a type of computer equipment but an exclusive restriction to handheld devices. This impression is reinforced by the manual's provision of only two examples for application of Data Element 8, both of which address vehicular negligent manslaughter cases. In one, "the officer obtained the phone records of the driver and found a series of texts were sent and received immediately prior to the accident," so the guidance is to code "C = Computer Equipment (Handheld Devices)." In the other, the death occurs after a driver tries to evade a traffic stop for speeding, but the driver is not observed using a cell phone, hence the guidance to code N for Not Applicable (Federal Bureau of Investigation, 2020, pp. 77–78). More recent revisions of the manual have included the same language and examples (e.g., Federal Bureau of Investigation, 2023b).

Appendix D

Biographical Sketches of Panel Members and Principal Staff

HAL S. STERN (*Chair*) is distinguished professor of statistics at the University of California, Irvine (UCI). He presently serves as co-director of the multi-university Center for Statistics and Applications in Forensic Evidence, funded by the National Institute of Standards and Technology. Stern is also part of the leadership team at the Conte Center at UCI, funded by the National Institute of Mental Health, which is studying how early-life experiences, and especially early-life adversity, influence brain maturation and contribute to vulnerability to mental health problems throughout life. He is known for his extensive research on Bayesian statistical methods. Stern is a fellow of the American Association for the Advancement of Science, the American Statistical Association, and the Institute for Mathematical Statistics. He has a B.S. degree in mathematics from the Massachusetts Institute of Technology, with both M.S. and Ph.D. degrees in statistics from Stanford University. At the National Academies of Sciences, Engineering, and Medicine, Stern was co-chair of the Panel on Research Methodologies and Statistical Approaches to Understanding Driver Fatigue Factors in Motor Carrier Safety and Driver Health, and chair of the Panel on Assessing the Benefits of the American Community Survey for the National Science Foundation's Division of Science Resources Statistics.

LYNN A. ADDINGTON is professor of justice, law, and criminology at American University (AU). Her research focuses on fatal and nonfatal victimization and includes post-victimization responses by victims, criminal justice actors, and service providers. Addington's research also reflects her extensive work with national crime data sources collected by the Federal

Bureau of Investigation, Bureau of Justice Statistics (BJS), National Center for Education Statistics, and Centers for Disease Control and Prevention. Her current work focuses on older adults and violent crime. Addington's most recent research has been funded by the National Institute of Justice. She is a past editor of *Homicide Studies*, and she continues to serve on its editorial board. Addington was a visiting fellow at the BJS, and she received AU's top award for faculty research. She has a Ph.D. in criminal justice from the University at Albany, State University of New York, and a J.D. from the University of Pennsylvania Law School. Beginning August 6, 2024, she was a paid consultant for BJS, working with its contractor Westat to review specific draft questionnaire items related to cybercrime concepts for possible inclusion in supplements to the National Crime Victimization Survey.

DANIEL L. CORK (*Study Director*) is a senior program officer for the Committee on National Statistics at the National Academies of Sciences, Engineering, and Medicine. He has served as study director or program officer for almost all census- or American Community Survey-related studies, including the Panels on Residence Rules in the Decennial Census and Research on Future Census Methods (2010 planning panel); the Standing Committee on Reengineering Census Operations; and the panels tasked with evaluating the quality of the 2000, 2010, and 2020 Censuses. He also directed the Panel to Review the Programs of the Bureau of Justice Statistics and the Panel on Modernizing the Nation's Crime Statistics (in cooperation with the Committee on Law and Justice); was senior program officer for the Committee to Assess the Feasibility, Accuracy, and Technical Capability of a National Ballistics Database (joint with the Committee on Law and Justice and the National Materials Advisory Board); and contributed to the work of the Committee on Best Practices for Assessing Mortality and Significant Morbidity Following Large-Scale Disasters (Board on Health Sciences Policy). His research interests include quantitative criminology, geographical analysis, Bayesian statistics, and statistics in sports. He has a B.S. in statistics from George Washington University and an M.S. in statistics and a joint Ph.D. in statistics and public policy from Carnegie Mellon University.

ERICA R. FISSEL is the research and evaluation manager at ICF, a global advisory and technology services provider. Prior to this, she was assistant professor in the Department of Criminal Justice at the University of Central Florida, with a secondary appointment with the Violence Against Women Research Cluster. Fissel's primary research interests focus on interpersonal cybercrimes, including cyberstalking, intimate partner cyber abuse, and cyberbullying. More specifically, her research explores theoretical correlates and causes of victimization and perpetration, post-victimization experiences, and public perceptions of cyber-based forms of abuse. She recently received two awards from divisions of the American Society of Criminology, acknowledging her contributions to the fields of victimology and cybercrime with the award for faculty researcher of the year (by the Division of Victimology) and early career researcher (by the Division of Cybercrime). Fissel has a Ph.D. in criminal justice from the University of Cincinnati. Beginning August 6, 2024, she was a paid consultant for the Bureau of Justice Statistics, working with its contractor Westat to review specific draft questionnaire items related to cybercrime concepts for possible inclusion in supplements to the National Crime Victimization Survey.

THOMAS J. HOLT is a professor in the School of Criminal Justice at Michigan State University and fellow in the cybercrime cluster at the Netherlands Institute for the Study of Crime and Law Enforcement. His research focuses on cybercrime, cyberterrorism, and the policy response to these issues, with particular emphasis on computer hacking, malicious software infections, data breaches and theft, online illicit market operations, and police preparedness to respond to cybercrime. Holt has published over 100 peer-reviewed articles on these issues in myriad outlets, including *British Journal of Criminology*, *Criminology and Public Policy*, *Crime and Delinquency*, *IEEE Security and Privacy*, *Social Science Computer Review*, and *Terrorism and Political Violence*. His research on under-reported forms of cybercrime and online extremist activity has been funded by the Department of Homeland Security, the National Institute of Justice, and the National Science Foundation, as well as the Australian Institute of Criminology and the Australian Research Council. Holt is a member of the American Society of Criminology and the European Society of Criminology and received the outstanding contribution award from the American Society of Criminology's Division of Cybercrime. He has a Ph.D. in criminology and criminal justice from the University of Missouri–St. Louis. Beginning August 6, 2024, he was a paid consultant for the Bureau of Justice Statistics, working with its contractor Westat to review specific draft questionnaire items related to cybercrime concepts for possible inclusion in supplements to the National Crime Victimization Survey.

JIN REE LEE is assistant professor in the Department of Criminology, Law and Society at George Mason University. He is also an affiliated research partner at Michigan State University's International Interdisciplinary Research Consortium on Cybercrime, George Mason University's Center for Evidence-Based Crime Policy, Boston University's Center for Cybercrime Investigation and Cybersecurity, and the University of Ontario Institute of Technology's Digital Life Research Group. Lee's work has examined various topics around cybercrime and cybersecurity, including law enforcement competencies and perceptions of online crime; computer hacking and the role of the internet in facilitating all manner of crime and deviance; online illicit market behaviors; ideologically motivated cyberattacks; and online interpersonal violence offending and victimization. His recent work has appeared in numerous peer-reviewed journals, including *Criminology and Public Policy, American Journal of Criminal Justice, Computers in Human Behavior, Crime and Delinquency, Journal of Interpersonal Violence, Terrorism, and Political Violence*, and *Victims and Offenders*. Lee is a recipient of the American Society of Criminology Division of Cybercrime Early Career Award. He has a Ph.D. in criminal justice from Michigan State University. Beginning August 6, 2024, he was a paid consultant for the Bureau of Justice Statistics, working with its contractor Westat to review specific draft questionnaire items related to cybercrime concepts for possible inclusion in supplements to the National Crime Victimization Survey.

DAVID MAIMON is a professor and a next-generation scholar in the Andrew Young School of Policy Studies' Department of Criminal Justice and Criminology, and he directs the Evidence-Based Cybersecurity Research Group at Georgia State University. He is also a research associate at the Hebrew University of Jerusalem's Federmann Cyber-Security Research Center. Maimon's research interests include theories of human behaviors, cyber-enabled and cyber-dependent crimes, and experimental research methods. His current research focuses on computer hacking and the progression of system-trespassing events, computer network vulnerabilities to cyberattacks, and decision-making processes in cyberspace. He also conducts research on intellectual property and cyber fraud. Maimon's research has been funded by grants from both government and private agencies in the United States and abroad. He received the Young Scholar Award from the White-Collar Crime Research Consortium of the National White-Collar Crime Center for his cybercrime research, the Philip Merrill Presidential Scholars Faculty Mentor Award from the University of Maryland, and the Best Publication Award in Mental Health from the American Sociological Association. Maimon has a Ph.D. in sociology from the Ohio State University.

MARIE-HELEN (MARIA) MARAS is a tenured full professor and the director of the Center for Cybercrime Studies at John Jay College of Criminal Justice. She is currently the director and principal investigator of approximately $3,100,000 in awards from the Bureau of Justice Assistance. Previously, Maras served as the director and principal investigator of a recently completed grant project on darknet fentanyl trafficking for the National Institute of Justice ($598,637) and served as a co-principal investigator on two recently completed National Science Foundation grants

($399,000) on improving cyberinfrastructure at the college and enhancing institutional cybersecurity research talent. Her academic background and research cover the topics of cybercrime, cybersecurity, and the impact of digital technology. Maras serves as a subject matter expert and consultant on cybercrime and cyber–organized crime for the United Nations Office on Drugs and Crime. She is the author of numerous peer-reviewed academic journal articles and books, including *Cybercriminology* (Oxford University Press) and *Computer Forensics: Cybercriminals, Laws, and Evidence* (Jones and Bartlett), among other books. Prior to her academic post, Maras served in the U.S. Navy, gaining significant experience in security, international investigations, and law enforcement. She has a Ph.D. in law and M.Sc. and M.Phil. degrees in criminology and criminal justice from the University of Oxford. Beginning August 6, 2024, she was a paid consultant for the Bureau of Justice Statistics, working with its contractor Westat to review specific draft questionnaire items related to cybercrime concepts for possible inclusion in supplements to the National Crime Victimization Survey.

MICHAEL C. MILLER is chief of police for the Colleyville Police Department in Texas. Prior to this, he served as assistant chief of police for the Coral Gables Police Department in Florida; in the Federal Bureau of Investigation (FBI) as a special assistant to the executive assistant director of the Criminal, Cyber, Response and Services Branch; as a special advisor to the assistant director of the Directorate of Intelligence; and as a detailee to the U.S. Bureau of Indian Affairs as deputy associate director of law enforcement operations. Prior to his positions at the FBI, he worked as a management consulting executive, where he held several positions focusing on public safety and law enforcement, most notably as the global program executive for Accenture's Immigration, Justice & Public Safety practice. Miller has a B.S. degree in biomedical science from Texas A&M University, where he was named an Outstanding Alumnus from the School of Veterinary Medicine and Biomedical Sciences, and an M.P.A. from Harvard University's John F. Kennedy School of Government. He is currently pursuing an M.S. degree in criminology and criminal justice from Texas Christian University. At the National Academies of Sciences, Engineering, and Medicine, Miller served on the Panel on Modernizing the Nation's Crime Statistics.

OJMARRH MITCHELL is a professor in the Department of Criminology, Law and Society at the University of California, Irvine. His research interests center on criminal justice policy, particularly in the areas of drug control, sentencing and corrections, and racial/ethnic fairness in the criminal justice system. Relating to his research on examining and understanding racial/ethnic disparities in the justice system, Mitchell received the Western

Society of Criminology's W.E.B. Du Bois award and both of the National Institute of Justice's W.E.B. Du Bois awards. He has served in numerous advisory roles, including on the U.S. Department of Justice's Science Advisory Board, New York City's Pretrial Research Advisory Council, Philadelphia's Pretrial Reform Advisory Council, and the American Society of Criminology's Executive Board. Mitchell serves as the vice president-elect of the American Society of Criminology and as the editor-in-chief for the journal *Criminology and Public Policy*. He has a B.A. in sociology from the University of Washington, with both M.A. and Ph.D. degrees in criminology and criminal justice from the University of Maryland.

ALEXIS R. PIQUERO is professor of sociology and criminology in the College of Arts and Sciences and distinguished scholar at the University of Miami. He previously served as director of the Bureau of Justice Statistics. Piquero is a nationally and internationally recognized criminologist. Throughout his career, he has given congressional testimony on evidence-based crime prevention practices and has provided counsel and support to several local, state, national, and international criminal justice agencies and elected leaders. Piquero's expertise ranges from criminal careers to criminal justice policy and crime prevention to the intersection of race/ethnicity and crime, with a focus on quantitative methodology. He has published over 500 scholarly articles and several books and is among the most highly cited criminologists in the world. Piquero is a fellow of the American Society of Criminology and the Academy of Criminal Justice Sciences. He received the Academy of Criminal Justice Sciences' Bruce Smith Sr. Award for outstanding contributions to criminal justice, and the Lifetime Achievement Award from the Division of Developmental and Life-Course Criminology of the American Society of Criminology. Piquero has a Ph.D. in criminology and criminal justice from the University of Maryland, College Park. At the National Academies of Sciences, Engineering, and Medicine, he served as member of the Panel on Modernizing the Nation's Crime Statistics as well as the Panels on Reviewing the Research Portfolio of the National Institute of Justice, Committee on a Prioritized Plan to Implement a Developmental Approach in Juvenile Justice Reform, and the Committee on Assessing the Research Program of the National Institute of Justice.

KATRINA BAUM STONE is a senior program officer for the Committee on National Statistics at the National Academies of Sciences, Engineering, and Medicine. Earlier in her career she worked on the development of the first supplements to the National Crime Victimization Survey to measure identity theft and stalking, as well as revisions to the School Crime Supplement. She has also worked with multiple federal agencies as a contractor or public servant including as government program director for J.D. Power, an expert appointee at the U.S. Peace Corps, and more than a decade at the U.S. Department of Justice as a senior statistician in the Bureau of Justice Statistics and senior research officer at the National Institute of Justice. Her research focuses on risk and resilience for vulnerable populations such as children, veterans, and survivors of sexual assault, stalking, and human trafficking. She served on the Federal Interagency Forum on Child and Family Statistics and as a founding member on the Institute of Medicine's Forum on Global Violence Prevention. While at the National Academies, she served as study director for a systematic review on alcohol and health and assisted studies of the 2020 Census as well as measuring sex, gender identity, and sexual orientation. She has a B.A. in law and society from University of California, Santa Barbara; an M.S. in criminal justice from Northeastern University; and a Ph.D. in social welfare from the University of Pennsylvania.

STACEY A. WRIGHT is director of Cyber Threat Intelligence (CTI) at CyberWA and teaches graduate courses at the University of Albany. Prior to this, she led a Cybersecurity & Infrastructure Security Agency cooperative agreement to incorporate state and local government requirements into the National Information Exchange Model Cyber Domain. Wright's career includes serving as the director of CTI for the Center for Internet Security's Multi-State Information Sharing and Analysis Center, as a cyber intelligence analyst at the Federal Bureau of Investigation's Albany office, and as an information technology specialist for the Cambridge Public Safety departments. Her industry work includes co-chairing the International Association of Chiefs of Police (IACP) Cyber Security Working Group and co-founding the Cyber Classification Compendium, which crosswalks cyber laws between the states and the American, Canadian, and Irish governments and is the foundation of the Canadian cybercrime reporting statistical model. She maintains engaged membership on the IACP's Cybercrime and Digital Evidence Committee and Criminal Justice Information System Security Policy Modernization Working Group, the National Sheriff's Association Cybersecurity and Crime Work Group, and IJIS Institute's Cyber Security Task Force. Wright is a published author, international speaker, and formally trained intelligence analyst. She has an M.B.A. from the University of Massachusetts, Boston.

COMMITTEE ON NATIONAL STATISTICS

The Committee on National Statistics was established in 1972 at the National Academies of Sciences, Engineering, and Medicine to improve the statistical methods and information on which public policy decisions are based. The committee carries out studies, workshops, and other activities to foster better measures and fuller understanding of the economy, the environment, public health, crime, education, immigration, poverty, welfare, and other public policy issues. It also evaluates ongoing statistical programs and tracks the statistical policy and coordinating activities of the federal government, serving a unique role at the intersection of statistics and public policy. The committee's work is supported by a consortium of federal agencies through a National Science Foundation grant, a National Agricultural Statistics Service cooperative agreement, and several individual contracts.